SMITHSONIAN
Presidents
and First Ladies

DK SMITHSONIAN ☀

Presidents

and First Ladies

Written by James Barber and Amy Pastan

DK Publishing, Inc.

LONDON, NEW YORK, MUNICH,
MELBOURNE, AND DELHI

MEDIA PROJECTS INC.
Executive Editor C. Carter Smith
Managing Editor Carter Smith
Project Editor Kathleen Feeley
Designer Laura Smyth

DK PUBLISHING, INC.
Editor Beth Sutinis
Art Editor Megan Clayton
Creative Director Tina Vaughan
Jacket Art Director Dirk Kaufman
Publisher Andrew Berkhut
Production Manager Chris Avgherinos

First American Edition, 2002
2 4 6 8 10 9 7 5 3 1

Published in the United States
by DK Publishing, Inc.
375 Hudson Street
New York, New York 10014

A catalog record for this book is available from the Library of Congress.

ISBN 0-7894-8453-6 (PB) 0-7894-8454-4 (HC)

Reproduced by Colourscan, Singapore
Printed and bound in Italy
by Graphicom, srl.

see our complete product line at
www.dk.com

CONTENTS

WASHINGTON

GEORGE WASHINGTON was sworn in as the first president of the newly formed United States of America in 1789. The American colonies had won independence from Great Britain in the Revolutionary War. As the hero of the war, Washington was everyone's first choice to be president. Washington displayed wisdom and moderation in launching the new United States' government and defined the presidency for all time.

REVOLUTIONARY LEADERSHIP

As a young man, Washington was made commander of the colonial army in Virginia. When the Revolutionary War against Britain began in 1775, Washington was chosen as commander of the American forces. Using common sense and determination, Washington held his badly equipped army together. He finally secured victory in 1781.

Compass belonging to Washington

BIOGRAPHY

★ 1ST PRESIDENT 1789–1797
★ BORN Westmoreland County, Va., Feb. 22, 1732
★ INAUGURATED AS PRESIDENT
First term: Apr. 30, 1789
Second term: Mar. 4, 1793
★ PARTY Federalist
★ DIED Mount Vernon, Va., Dec. 14, 1799, age 67

KEY EVENTS

1749 Martha Dandridge marries Daniel Parke Custis.
1752 George Washington inherits Mount Vernon.
1757 Daniel Custis dies.
1759 Washington and Martha Dandridge Custis are married; Martha has two children from her first marriage that George adopts.
1774 Washington is a delegate at the First Continental Congress.
1775 Revolutionary War begins with the Battles at Lexington and Concord; Washington is chosen commander of the American forces.
1776 The Declaration of Independence is written; Washington's troops cross the Delaware River and win a key battle at Trenton, New Jersey.

MARTHA WASHINGTON

America's initial first lady was a dignified woman who understood the importance of her role. Martha's first husband died after eight years of marriage, leaving her with two small children and a large inheritance. During the Revolutionary War, she followed her second husband, General George Washington, from camp to camp. Like many women, Martha risked her own safety to visit her soldier–husband. She also nursed the sick and organized relief efforts during the war. When Washington became president, Martha managed their household and hosted official functions with decorum and grace.

BIOGRAPHY

★ **YEARS AS FIRST LADY**
1789–1797
★ **BORN** New Kent County, Va., June 2, 1731
★ **MARRIED** New Kent County, Va., Jan. 6, 1759
★ **CHILDREN** (from former marriage) John Parke Custis, Martha Parke Custis
★ **DIED** Mount Vernon, Va., May 22, 1802, age 70

George and Martha Washington with two of their grandchildren

KEY EVENTS

1777 Congress adopts the Articles of Confederation.
1778 Martha Washington visits her husband at his army camp in Valley Forge, Pennsylvania.
1781 British General Cornwallis surrenders to

Washington at Yorktown.
1782 Martha visits colonial soldiers camped at Newburgh, New York.
1783 The American Revolution ends.
1787 Washington leads the convention in Philadelphia where the U.S.

Constitution is drafted.
1788 After fierce debate in many states, the Constitution is ratified.
1789 At the first session of Congress, Washington is elected president; he appoints Thomas Jefferson secretary of state.

THE NEW PRESIDENT

George Washington's powers as president were set out clearly under the new Constitution. It was his responsibility to make sure that the laws of the land were followed and to appoint high-ranking government officials and judges. He also had the power to command the armed forces and to make treaties with other countries. Washington was so admired by the people that he probably could have been president for as long as he wished. But the Constitution stated that each president should serve a four-year term of office and then stand for reelection. Washington did this and, after two terms, he decided that he had served long enough.

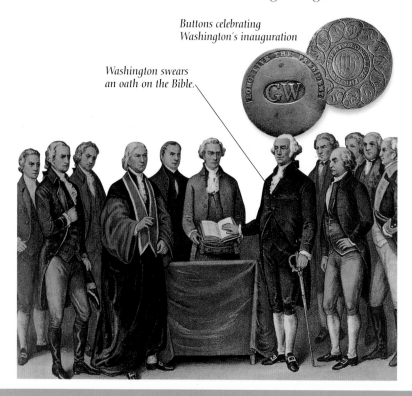

Buttons celebrating Washington's inauguration

Washington swears an oath on the Bible.

KEY EVENTS

1789 Alexander Hamilton is appointed secretary of treasury; John Adams is vice president.
1790 Supreme Court meets for first time.
1791 A national bank is established; the site for the nation's new capital,

Washington D.C., is selected; the first ten amendments of the Constitution are ratified.
1792 Congress establishes a national mint; Washington is reelected president.
1793 Washington issues the Proclamation of

Neutrality to avoid conflict with Great Britain and France, who are at war; Jefferson resigns as secretary of state.
1794 Washington sends Supreme Court Justice John Jay to England to negotiate the unpopular

MOUNT VERNON

At the age of 20, George Washington inherited the Mount Vernon estate and became one of the largest landowners in northern Virginia. He improved the house and gradually added new land to the estate until it covered over 8,000 acres. He experimented with new ways of improving his crops and livestock, and he especially enjoyed planting trees, several of which still tower over the estate today. He loved farming, regarding it as "the most noble employment of man." After leaving the White House, he and Martha entertained the hundreds of guests who visited Mount Vernon every year.

U.S. banknote, 1800

THE LEGEND OF GEORGE WASHINGTON

George Washington became a legend in his own lifetime. He had endured the trials of fighting a war and forging a nation, and his virtues became associated with the character of the new republic. He was called the "Father of His Country" and his image soon began to appear on everything from porcelain to banknotes. After his death, the story of his life was retold and embellished by admiring writers and poets.

KEY EVENTS

Jay Treaty, allowing U.S. ships to be inspected at sea in return for the removal of British troops from the Northwest Territory; Washington puts down the Whiskey Rebellion when farmers in Pennsylvania refuse to pay a new federal whiskey tax. **1795** Northwest Indians sign the Treaty of Fort Greenville, giving most of Ohio to the U.S. government. **1796** Washington declines to serve a third term; John Adams defeats Thomas Jefferson in a close presidential election. **1797** George and Martha Washington retire to Mount Vernon. **1799** George Washington dies. **1802** Martha Washington dies.

ADAMS

JOHN ADAMS was not a popular hero like George Washington. Yet he was one of the great Founding Fathers of the United States. Adams helped draft the Declaration of Independence and also served as a diplomat in Europe. Foreign affairs dominated his presidency, especially the war between Great Britain and France. To his credit, Adams kept the United States out of the conflict. His wife, Abigail, was the first to be the wife of one U.S. president and mother of another: John Quincy Adams.

HIS ROTUNDITY

By his own admission, Adams was "puffy, vain, conceited," and as Washington's vice president, he encouraged the Senate to bestow grand titles on members of the new government. As a result, Adam's enemies began calling him "His Rotundity."

Vest belonging to John Adams

BIOGRAPHY

★ **2ND PRESIDENT**
1797–1801
★ **BORN** Braintree (now Quincy), Mass., Oct. 30, 1735
★ **INAUGURATED AS PRESIDENT**
Mar. 4, 1797
★ **PARTY** Federalist
★ **DIED** Quincy, Mass., July 4, 1826, age 90

KEY EVENTS

1764 John Adams and Abigail Smith marry.
1776 Adams helps draft the Declaration of Independence.
1780 John Adams writes the Massachusetts state constitution.
1783 Adams helps

negotiate the treaty that ends the American Revolution.
1785 Adams serves as American minister to Great Britain.
1789 Adams becomes Washington's vice president and serves for two terms.

1797 After a bitter and close election, Adams takes office with Thomas Jefferson as vice president; the French government breaks off diplomatic relations with the U.S. and begins attacking U.S. ships.
1798 Congress votes to

FATHER OF THE NAVY

When Adams became president, Great Britain and France were at war. Although the United States was neutral, France attacked U.S. ships to prevent trading with Great Britain. War with France seemed imminent, so Adams established a naval department and ordered warships to be built. War was never officially declared, though French and U.S. ships engaged in battle at sea. In 1800, Adams negotiated an end to the hostilities.

ABIGAIL ADAMS

Her extraordinary intelligence, love of learning, and keen interest in politics made Abigail Adams the perfect partner for her ambitious husband. She is one of the few first ladies known for her own accomplishments. During the Revolutionary War, Mrs. Adams ran the family farm, as cannon fire erupted not far from her doorstep. She was a true patriot who supported and influenced her husband, urging him to "remember the ladies." John's political rivals called the opinionated Abigail "Mrs. President," implying that she had too much political influence over him.

BIOGRAPHY

★ **YEARS AS FIRST LADY** 1797–1801
★ **BORN** Weymouth, Mass., Nov. 23, 1744
★ **MARRIED** Weymouth, Mass., Oct. 25, 1764
★ **CHILDREN** Abigail Amelia, John Quincy, Susanna, Charles, Thomas Boylston
★ **DIED** Quincy, Mass., Oct. 28, 1818, age 73

KEY EVENTS

enlarge the army and navy; an unofficial naval war between France and the United States begins.
1799 Adams sends troops into Pennsylvania to force farmers to pay a new federal land tax.
1800 John Adams and his family move into the unfinished presidential residence in the new capital, Washington, D.C.; Spain gives the Louisiana Territory back to France.
1801 Abigail Adams opens the White House to visitors on New Year's Day; Thomas Jefferson is elected president after a close race; Adams appoints John Marshall chief justice of the Supreme Court; John and Abigail Adams retire to their Massachusetts home.
1818 Abigail Adams dies.
1826 John Adams dies.

JEFFERSON

THOMAS JEFFERSON believed in a national government that had limited powers over the states and the people. Yet as president, Jefferson made bold decisions. In 1803, he purchased the Louisiana territory from France, even though the Constitution did not authorize it. This doubled the size of the country and made westward expansion possible. Jefferson also kept the nation neutral during the Napoleonic Wars. After eight years as president, Jefferson stepped down because he believed that no leader should serve more than two terms.

Jefferson's writing desk

BIOGRAPHY

★ **3RD PRESIDENT** 1801–1809
★ **BORN** Albemarle, County, Va., Apr. 13, 1743
★ **INAUGURATED AS PRESIDENT** First term: Mar. 4, 1801 Second term: Mar. 4, 1805
★ **PARTY** Democratic–Republican
★ **DIED** Charlottesville, Va., July 4, 1826, age 83

JEFFERSON THE PATRIOT

At the start of the Revolutionary War, Jefferson served in the Continental Congress and wrote the Declaration of Independence. He was also elected governor of Virginia and served as Washington's secretary of state.

KEY EVENTS

1760 Thomas Jefferson enters the College of William and Mary.
1767 Jefferson begins to practice law.
1768 Jefferson begins building Monticello; Jefferson is elected to the Virginia legislature.

1772 Thomas Jefferson and Martha Wayles Skelton marry; their daughter Martha is born.
1774 Jefferson writes the political essay "A Summary View of the Rights of British America."
1775 Jefferson serves in

the Second Continental Congress.
1776 Jefferson writes the Declaration of Independence.
1779 Jefferson is elected governor of Virginia.
1781 Jefferson writes *Notes on the State of Virginia.*

MARTHA JEFFERSON

Martha Wayles Skelton was a young widow of considerable means when she met, and married, Thomas Jefferson. Though little is known about Martha and no portraits exist of her today, she and Jefferson shared a love of music and literature, and her husband later described his married life as "ten years of uncheckered happiness." Sadly, the difficult births of six children took their toll on Martha. She died at age thirty-three—nineteen years before Jefferson was elected president. After her death, Jefferson came to rely on his oldest daughter, also named Martha.

BIOGRAPHY

- ★ NEVER SERVED AS FIRST LADY
- ★ BORN Charles City County, Va., Oct. 30, 1748
- ★ MARRIED Charles City County, Va., Jan. 1, 1772
- ★ CHILDREN Martha, Mary, Lucy Elizabeth, two girls and one boy who died in infancy
- ★ DIED Charlottesville, Va., Sept. 6, 1782, age 33

Martha Jefferson Randolph

THE PRESIDENT'S OFFICIAL HOSTESS

In the nineteenth century, it was considered improper for women to attend a social event if only men were present. Since he never remarried, Jefferson asked Dolley Madison, a family friend and future first lady, as well as his daughter, Martha Jefferson Randolph, to preside over official festivities. Future presidents who did not have a wife followed this practice, choosing a female friend or relative to serve as official hostess. When Martha Jefferson Randolph sat for this portrait, she was a fifty-one-year-old mother of eleven children.

KEY EVENTS

1782 Martha Jefferson dies.
1784 Jefferson serves as American minister to France; Martha accompanies her father to France.
1789 French Revolution begins.

1790 Jefferson is appointed Washington's secretary of state.
1796 John Adams defeats Jefferson in the presidential election.
1798 Jefferson writes the "Virginia Resolutions," a defense of state's rights.

1800 In the 1800 election, Thomas Jefferson and Aaron Burr tie in the electoral college; Spain gives Louisiana back to France.
1801 The House of Representatives elects Jefferson to the presidency with Burr as vice president.

THE GREAT SCHOLAR

Thomas Jefferson was one of the most learned men in American history. He knew six different languages, studied

music, law, science, and philosophy, and was a talented, self-taught architect. Jefferson's accomplishments reflected his varied interests. Not only did he write the Declaration of Independence, he championed religious freedom and public education, dispatched an expedition to discover the natural wonders of the continent, and pioneered neoclassical architecture in the United States.

Declaration of Independence

THE LEWIS AND CLARK EXPEDITION

Jefferson was a keen amateur naturalist, and he was eager to find out about the American interior. In 1804, he sent an expedition, led by Meriwether Lewis and William Clark, to explore the newly acquired Louisiana Territory. Lewis and Clark were aided by a Shoshone girl named Sacagawea, who helped them communicate with the different Native American peoples they met. Over two years, the expedition members traveled as far as the Pacific Ocean. They kept detailed accounts of plants, animals, and birds they saw, as well as mapped the natural features of the continent.

Lewis and Clark's compass

KEY EVENTS

1801 Jefferson appoints James Madison secretary of state; Jefferson sends the navy to quell the Barbary pirates in the Mediterranean.
1802 Congress repeals all internal taxes.
1803 In the *Marbury v. Madison* case, the Supreme

Court declares an act of Congress to be unconstitutional for the first time; Jefferson makes the Louisiana Purchase.
1804 Jefferson is reelected president; the Lewis and Clark expedition sets off; Jefferson's rival,

Aaron Burr, kills Alexander Hamilton in a duel; the Twelfth Amendment is ratified, separating the election ballots for president and vice president.
1806 Burr tries to incite a rebellion in Louisiana.

MONTICELLO

One of Jefferson's many interests was architecture. Inspired by the work of the 16th-century Italian architect Andrea Palladio, he designed his own home on a hill above Charlottesville, Virginia. He named it Monticello, the Italian word for "little mountain." This elegant 32-room house was surrounded by beautiful gardens. It was the embodiment of Jefferson's classical tastes and learning. He designed many special features for Monticello, such as a dumbwaiter in which food and wine could be raised from the cellar, swivel chairs, alcove beds, and an elaborate parquet floor for the parlor. When Jefferson's presidency ended, he returned to Monticello with his daughter Martha Randolph and her children.

FINAL RESTING PLACE

Thomas Jefferson died on July 4, 1826, just a few hours before his fellow countryman John Adams. He was laid to rest at Monticello. Jefferson left an epitaph to be inscribed on his gravestone, which read: "Here was buried Thomas Jefferson, Author of the Declaration of Independence, of the Statute of Virginia for Religious Freedom, and the Father of the University of Virginia." Jefferson chose not to mention that he had also been president of the United States.

Snuffbox with image of Jefferson

KEY EVENTS

1807 Burr is arrested and tried for treason, but is acquitted; the U.S. frigate *Chesapeake* is fired upon and boarded by the British warship *Leopard*—Jefferson sticks to his policy of neutrality and avoids a declaration of war; Jefferson signs the Embargo Act banning the export of U.S. goods to Europe in retaliation for the *Chesapeake* incident.

1808 Jefferson prohibits the import of slaves from Africa; Jefferson does not run for a third term.

1809 The Embargo Act is repealed.
1819 Jefferson founds the University of Virginia.
1825 The University of Virginia opens.
1826 Thomas Jefferson dies on July 4, just a few hours before John Adams.

MADISON

JAMES MADISON was a great political thinker. In 1787, he was a leader in framing the U.S. Constitution. After serving as Jefferson's secretary of state, Madison became president in 1809. During his administration, the United States became involved in the War of 1812 with Great Britain. The war went badly for the United States, but Madison's reputation was rescued, in part, with a U.S. victory at the Battle of New Orleans in 1815.

BIOGRAPHY

★ **4TH PRESIDENT** 1809–1817
★ **BORN** Port Conway, Va., Mar. 16, 1751
★ **PARTY** Democratic–Republican
★ **DIED** Montpelier, Va., June 28, 1836, age 85

THE BILL OF RIGHTS

Madison felt that the Constitution did not do enough to protect the rights of individuals. He led the fight to have safeguards built into it. These became the first ten amendments, known as the Bill of Rights. Adopted in 1791, it guaranteed freedom of speech and religion and the right to trial by jury.

KEY EVENTS

1794 James Madison and Dolley Payne Todd marry.
1801 Jefferson appoints Madison secretary of state.
1808 Madison is elected president.
1810 Congress votes to resume U.S. trade with Great Britain and France.
1811 The first national bank of the United States closes its doors.
1812 British harassment of U.S. ships and the kidnapping of U.S. sailors leads Madison to declare war on Great Britain; Madison is reelected president.
1813 In the Battle of Lake Erie, U.S. naval forces led by Oliver Hazard Perry score an important victory in the war against Great Britain.

DOLLEY MADISON

Dolley Payne Todd married Virginia congressman James Madison less than a year after the death of her first husband. Before she became first lady, Dolley occasionally served as official hostess for Thomas Jefferson. On entering the President's House, she was already an experienced political wife and a leader of Washington society. The first lady, who had a warmth and vitality that drew people to her, blossomed in her new role. After James's death in 1836, she remained an important figure in the social circles of the nation's capital.

Dish used at Executive Mansion

BIOGRAPHY

★ **YEARS AS FIRST LADY**
1809–1817
★ **BORN** Guilford County, N.C., May 20, 1768
★ **MARRIED** Harewood, Va., Sept. 15, 1794
★ **CHILDREN** (from former marriage) Payne Todd
★ **DIED** Washington, D.C., July 12, 1849, age 81

SAVING THE NATION'S HERITAGE

During the War of 1812, British forces invaded and burned Washington D.C. As British troops were advancing on the capital, Dolley Madison was told to flee. In her husband's absence, she calmly packed up his papers, the national seal, and a portrait of George Washington, and left just before British troops set fire to the President's House. This daring act won her the everlasting admiration of the American public.

KEY EVENTS

1814 Washington D.C. is invaded and burned by British forces; Dolley Madison rescues valuable state documents just before the British set fire to the President's House; British attack on Fort McHenry in Baltimore Harbor inspires Francis Scott Key to compose "The Star-Spangled Banner"; later that year the United States and Great Britain sign a peace treaty ending the War of 1812.
1815 General Andrew Jackson wins a brilliant victory at the Battle of New Orleans.
1816 The Second Bank of the United States is chartered.
1836 James Madison dies.
1849 Dolley Madison dies.

MONROE

JAMES MONROE was the last of the Revolutionary patriots to become president. Serious by nature, Monroe proved to be a popular president. Monroe's presidency was known as the "Era of Good Feelings" because the nation was politically tranquil and at peace with other nations. Yet there was a depression in 1819, and the next year, the Missouri Compromise ignited debates about the extension of slavery in new states and territories. Monroe is best remembered, though, for his famous foreign policy doctrine.

Handwritten draft of Monroe Doctrine

THE MONROE DOCTRINE

In December, 1823, President Monroe announced his new foreign policy. He declared that the United States would not look kindly on European nations that interfered in North and South American affairs. He warned against any attempts to establish colonies in the Americas by European powers. This policy became known as the Monroe Doctrine.

BIOGRAPHY

★ **5TH PRESIDENT**
  1817–1825
★ **BORN** Westmoreland County, Va., Apr. 28, 1758
★ **PARTY** Democratic–Republican
★ **DIED** New York, N.Y., July 4, 1831, age 73

KEY EVENTS

1776 A lieutenant in the colonial army, James Monroe crosses the Delaware River with Washington's troops.
1786 Monroe and Elizabeth Kortright marry.
1790 Monroe is elected to U.S. Senate.

1794 Washington appoints Monroe minister to France.
1803 Monroe helps negotiate the Louisiana Purchase.
1811 Madison appoints Monroe secretary of state.
1816 Monroe is elected president.

1817 The Monroe family moves into the White House; Monroe appoints John Quincy Adams secretary of state; Great Britain and the U.S. limit naval forces on the Great Lakes to maintain peace at the U.S.-Canadian border.

ELIZABETH MONROE

As first lady, Elizabeth Monroe attended few formal functions; many interpreted her reserve as being aloof and haughty. Yet she played a key role in a diplomatic event while her husband was serving as U.S. minister to France after the French Revolution. During that period, the French imprisoned and executed those who remained loyal to their former king. One suspected of such loyalty was the Marquis de Lafayette, a Frenchman who had helped Americans fight in the Revolutionary War. Elizabeth dared visit Lafayette's wife when she was imprisoned—and as a result, saved her from being beheaded.

BIOGRAPHY

★ YEARS AS FIRST LADY 1817–1825
★ BORN New York, N.Y., June 30, 1768
★ MARRIED N.Y., N.Y., Feb. 16, 1786
★ CHILDREN Eliza, Maria Hester
★ DIED Oak Hill, Va., Sept. 23, 1830, age 62

THE "WHITE HOUSE"

During the War of 1812, the British had burned the President's House. By Monroe's administration, the Executive Mansion was rebuilt and painted white. Thereafter it became popularly known as the White House.

KEY EVENTS

1818 General Andrew Jackson invades Spanish Florida; the U.S. and Great Britain agree to joint control of the Oregon Territory.
1819 An economic depression strikes the nation; Florida is purchased from Spain; the Supreme Court rules that the second bank of the United States is constitutional.
1820 The Missouri Compromise is passed, maintaining the balance of power between free and slave states; Monroe is reelected president.

1823 The Monroe Doctrine is announced.
1825 James and Elizabeth Monroe retire to their Virginia home.
1830 Elizabeth Monroe dies.
1831 James Monroe dies.

ADAMS

JOHN QUINCY ADAMS was the son of former president John Adams. Like his father, John Quincy Adams had a sober personality. He was more interested in scholarly pursuits than in card playing and dancing. His education and talent for learning languages contributed to his great success as a diplomat. Yet as president, Adams was not as successful. He found that the people were not interested in his advanced ideas for spending their taxes on building roads and canals and doing scientific explorations. Adams was not reelected.

BIOGRAPHY

★ **6TH PRESIDENT** 1825–1829
★ **BORN** Quincy, Mass., July 11, 1767
★ **PARTY** National-Republican
★ **DIED** Washington, D.C., Feb. 23, 1848, age 80

Microscope belonging to Adams

DEATH IN THE HOUSE

John Quincy Adams did not retire from public office when he lost the election of 1828. Instead, he embarked on a long and distinguished career in the House of Representatives. In 1848, at the age of 80, Adams suffered a stroke while seated in the House. He was carried to the Speaker's Room, where he died two days later. His last words were: "Thank the officers of the House. This is the last of earth. I am content."

KEY EVENTS

1790 John Quincy Adams begins to practice law.
1794 Adams is appointed U.S. minister to the Netherlands; Adams meets Louisa Catherine Johnson in London.
1797 Adams and Johnson marry.

1803 Adams begins serving in U.S. Senate.
1806 Adams begins work as professor at Harvard College (now known as Harvard University).
1809 Adams is appointed U.S. minister to Russia.
1815 Adams is appointed

U.S. minister to England.
1817 Monroe appoints Adams secretary of state.
1823 Adams helps Monroe draft the Monroe Doctrine.
1824 Adams and Andrew Jackson run for president in a close race.

LOUISA ADAMS

The wife of John Quincy Adams disliked the demanding duties of first lady but rose to the task admirably. Born in England to a British mother and an American father, she discovered that the young diplomat she married was dour and inflexible. The disapproval of her mother-in-law, the formidable Abigail Adams, made matters worse. Yet the European manners to which the senior Mrs. Adams objected made Louisa the most popular and successful hostess of her era in Washington.

A THWARTED MUSICIAN

Although she was a talented singer and harpist, Louisa had only one career option: to marry well and have children. At the request of her husband, she stopped performing music for friends at social gatherings when she became first lady. Louisa felt trapped in the White House, which she called "a dull and stately prison." Her journals reveal the frustrations of a woman whose abilities were not allowed to flourish.

BIOGRAPHY

★ **YEARS AS FIRST LADY**
1825–1829
★ **BORN** London, England,
Feb. 12, 1775
★ **MARRIED** London, England,
July 26, 1797
★ **CHILDREN** George
Washington, John, Charles
Francis, Louisa Catherine
★ **DIED** Washington, D.C.,
May 15, 1852, age 77

KEY EVENTS

1825 The House of Representatives chooses Adams as president; Adams appoints Henry Clay secretary of state, leading to charges that Adams and Clay conspired to win the presidency for Adams; the Erie Canal is completed.

1828 The Tariff of Abominations is passed; Andrew Jackson defeats Adams in the presidential election.
1830 Adams is elected to U.S. House of Representatives and will serve there until his death.

1841 Adams wins the freedom of escaped slaves aboard the slave ship *Amistad.*
1848 John Quincy Adams has a stroke in House chambers and dies two days later.
1852 Louisa Adams dies.

JACKSON

ANDREW JACKSON was the first president to be born in a log cabin. Jackson, a former soldier, believed that as president it was his job to represent the interests of ordinary American citizens. He fought constantly with Congress and used his powers to veto legislation that he thought favored the wealthy elite. This policy became known as "Jacksonian democracy." Jackson's popularity with the voters soared and he was easily reelected.

Metal statuette of General Andrew Jackson

A BATTLEFIELD HERO FOR PRESIDENT

Andrew Jackson rose from poverty to become a prosperous planter and a judge. He also had a legendary military career. He became known as the "Hero of New Orleans" for defeating the British army in the War of 1812. Jackson was the second battlefield hero to become president; George Washington was the first.

BIOGRAPHY

★ **7TH PRESIDENT** 1829–1837
★ **BORN** The Waxhaws, S.C., Mar. 15, 1767
★ **INAUGURATED AS PRESIDENT** First term: Mar. 4, 1829
Second term: Mar. 4, 1833
★ **PARTY** Democratic
★ **DIED** Nashville, Tenn., June 8, 1845, age 78

KEY EVENTS

1787 Andrew Jackson begins to practice law.
1785 Rachel Donelson and Louis Robards marry.
1790 Rachel and Louis Robards separate and prepare to divorce.
1791 Andrew Jackson and Rachel Donelson

Robards marry.
1794 The Jacksons have a second marriage ceremony after discovering that Rachel's divorce from her first husband was not final in 1791.
1796 Jackson is elected to U.S. Senate.

1798 Jackson is appointed to Tennessee Supreme Court.
1815 U.S. troops under then-General Jackson win a decisive victory in the Battle of New Orleans during the War of 1812.
1825 Jackson is defeated

FORCING THE INDIANS WEST

As a frontier general, Jackson fought in the Revolutionary War with the Creek Indians. The Creeks called him "Sharp Knife," a name Jackson lived up to. As president, he signed the Indian Removal Act (1830). This allowed the government to forcibly remove Native Americans from their eastern homelands to the frontier, west of the Mississippi River.

RACHEL JACKSON

Rachel married Andrew Jackson in 1791 after divorcing her jealous, abusive first husband, Louis Robards. Then she discovered that her divorce from Robards was not final. The matter was corrected in 1794, but it surfaced again in 1828 when Jackson's political foes started rumors that Rachel was a bigamist—a person with more than one spouse—to discredit Andrew. The scandal took its toll on Rachel. She died of a heart attack only five days after Andrew won the 1828 election. Jackson's niece Emily Donelson and daughter-in-law Sarah Yorke Jackson served as official hostesses during his administration.

BIOGRAPHY

★ NEVER SERVED AS FIRST LADY
★ BORN Halifax County, Va., June 15, 1767
★ CHILDREN Andrew (adopted)
★ DIED Nashville, Tenn., Dec. 22, 1828, age 61

KEY EVENTS

by John Quincy Adams in a close presidential race.
1828 Andrew Jackson is elected president; Rachel Jackson dies of a heart attack.
1829 Jackson's inaugural celebration becomes so rowdy that he is forced to flee the White House.
1830 Jackson signs the Indian Removal Act.
1832 Jackson is reelected president, with Martin Van Buren as vice president.
1835 The Texas Revolution begins when Texas settlers rebel against the Mexican government.
1836 In the siege of the Alamo, the Texas rebel forces are defeated, but a few weeks later, Texas wins its independence from Mexico.
1845 Andrew Jackson dies.

VAN BUREN

MARTIN VAN BUREN

inspired the nickname "Little Magician," which referred to his political skills. Van Buren had been Andrew Jackson's trusted vice president. Jackson chose his friend to be the next president, and the voters supported Jackson's choice. Unfortunately, a severe economic depression followed Van Buren into the White House. When he could not find a solution to bring back prosperity, he was voted out of office.

BIOGRAPHY

★ 8TH PRESIDENT
1837–1841
★ BORN Kinderhook, N.Y.,
Dec. 5, 1782
★ PARTY Democratic
★ DIED Kinderhook, N.Y.,
July 24, 1862, age 79

HANNAH VAN BUREN

Hannah Hoes and Martin Van Buren were cousins who grew

BIOGRAPHY

★ NEVER SERVED AS
FIRST LADY
★ BORN Kinderhook,
N.Y., Mar. 8, 1783
★ DIED Albany, N.Y.,
Feb. 5, 1819, age 35

up together and eventually married. Little is known about Hannah, who died of tuberculosis in 1819. Van Buren never remarried, so his daughter-in-law, Angelica Singleton Van Buren, served as official White House hostess.

KEY EVENTS

1807 Martin Van Buren and Hannah Hoes marry.
1819 Hannah Van Buren dies.
1832 Van Buren is elected vice president.
1836 Van Buren is elected president after a close race.

1838 Van Buren's son, Abraham, marries Angelica Singleton, who serves as the official White House hostess.
1838–1839 Fifteen thousand Cherokee are forced to leave their Georgia homeland and relocate on reservations in the West;

about 4,000 Cherokee die on the journey known as the "Trail of Tears."
1840 William Henry Harrison defeats Van Buren in the presidential election.
1862 Martin Van Buren dies.

HARRISON

WILLIAM HENRY HARRISON

grew up on a Virginia plantation and was a military hero. In 1811, he defeated Tecumseh and his Shawnee warriors at the Battle of Tippecanoe in the Indiana Territory. Harrison's father signed the Declaration of Independence and his grandson, Benjamin Harrison, would later become president. Harrison is remembered largely for serving the shortest term of any president. A month after he was inaugurated, he died of pneumonia.

BIOGRAPHY
- ★ 9TH PRESIDENT
  Mar. 4–Apr. 4, 1841
- ★ BORN Berkeley, Va.,
  Feb. 9, 1773
- ★ PARTY Whig
- ★ DIED Washington, D.C.,
  Apr. 4, 1841, age 68

BIOGRAPHY
- ★ SERVED AS FIRST
  LADY Mar. 4–
  Apr. 4 1841
- ★ BORN
  Morristown, N.J.,
  July 25, 1775
- ★ DIED North Bend,
  Ohio, Feb. 25, 1864,
  age 88

ANNA HARRISON

Anna Symmes Harrison had been delayed joining her husband in the nation's capital due to the sudden death of one of their sons. She was still packing for the journey when she learned of her husband's untimely death.

KEY EVENTS

1795 William Henry Harrison and Anna Symmes marry.
1800 Harrison is elected governor of the Indiana Territory.
1813 Harrison wins a decisive victory at the Battle of Thames in the War of 1812.
1824 Harrison is elected to U.S. Senate.
1840 Harrison is elected president.
1841 Harrison dies one month after his inauguration, becoming the first president to die while in office; Vice President John Tyler becomes president.
1864 Anna Harrison dies.
1888 Benjamin Harrison, grandson of William and Anna, is elected president.

TYLER

JOHN TYLER became the first vice president to be made president of the United States after the death of a sitting president. Tyler belonged to the Whig Party, but he did not support many things the Whigs believed in. Worse still, Tyler supported slavery, which many Whigs denounced. He became an outcast in his own party. Many of Tyler's critics challenged his right to call himself president because he had not been elected. When Tyler remarried after the death of his first wife, he became the first president to be married while in office.

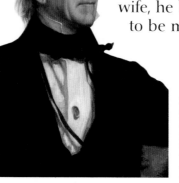

Tyler pamphlet

BIOGRAPHY

★ **10TH PRESIDENT** 1841–1845
★ **BORN** Charles City County, Va., Mar. 29, 1790
★ **PARTY** Whig
★ **DIED** Richmond, Va., Jan. 18, 1862, age 71

A TRUE PRESIDENT

Many of Tyler's foes referred to him as "His Accidency," and he proudly refused to open any mail addressed to the "Acting President." Tyler set an important precedent for future vice presidents who became president, because he steadfastly exercised all of the powers and privileges of the presidency.

KEY EVENTS

1807 John Tyler graduates from the College of William and Mary.
1813 John Tyler and Letitia Christian marry.
1816 Tyler is elected to U.S. House of Representatives.

1823 Tyler enters Virginia state legislature.
1825 Tyler becomes governor of Virginia.
1827 Tyler becomes a U.S. senator from Virginia.
1836 Tyler resigns his Senate seat rather than change his vote as directed

by his party.
1839 Letitia Tyler suffers a stroke.
1840 William Henry Harrison is elected president with John Tyler as his vice president.
1841 Harrison dies and Tyler becomes president;

LETITIA TYLER

Letitia Tyler married John Tyler just after he was elected to the Virginia state legislature. Although a stroke she suffered in 1839 left her partially paralyzed, she moved to Washington after John became vice president in 1841. When he took over the presidency, Letitia found that she had to yield the duties of first lady to her daughter-in-law Priscilla. Mrs. Tyler had a second stroke on September 10, 1842, and died in the White House partway through John's presidential term.

BIOGRAPHY

★ **YEARS AS FIRST LADY**
1841–1842
★ **BORN** New Kent County, Va., Nov. 12, 1790
★ **DIED** Washington D.C., Sept. 10, 1842, age 51

JULIA TYLER

Following Letitia's death, John soon remarried. Julia Tyler was a vivacious twenty-four year old who became the talk of Washington. At boarding school, she had sparked a scandal by modeling for an advertisement. Her parents whisked her away to Europe and then to Washington, D.C., where she met and married Tyler. She spent only a few months as first lady but delved into her role with enthusiasm.

BIOGRAPHY

★ **YEARS AS FIRST LADY**
1844–1845
★ **BORN** Gardiner's Island, N.Y., May 4, 1820
★ **DIED** Richmond, Va., July 10, 1889, age 69

KEY EVENTS

most of Tyler's cabinet resigns after he vetoes bills to re-establish a national bank; Congress passes a pre-emption bill, giving squatters the right to settle on unsurveyed federal land.
1842 Letitia Tyler dies; U.S. and Great Britain finally

establish the border between Maine and Canada with the Webster-Ashburton Treaty.
1844 John Tyler and Julia Gardiner marry; Mormon leader Joseph Smith is murdered by a mob; Tyler withdraws from the

presidential race; James K. Polk is elected to the presidency.
1861 Tyler comes out of retirement to chair a conference to resolve the crisis over slavery.
1862 John Tyler dies.
1889 Julia Tyler dies.

POLK

JAMES K. POLK was a former speaker of the House of Representatives and a governor of Tennessee, but few people saw him as a presidential candidate. However, Polk proved to be a diligent worker. He believed that the United States should fulfill its "manifest destiny" of expanding westward to the Pacific Ocean. In 1846, a border dispute in the new state of Texas triggered a war with Mexico. After the war, the victorious Americans acquired California and New Mexico. When Polk left office, the country reached from ocean to ocean.

BIOGRAPHY

★ **11TH PRESIDENT**
1845–1849

★ **BORN** Mecklenburg County, N.C., Nov. 2, 1795

★ **INAUGURATED AS PRESIDENT** March 4, 1845

★ **PARTY** Democratic

★ **DIED** Nashville, Tenn., June 15, 1849, age 53

Colt revolver

THE MEXICAN WAR

When Mexico turned down Polk's offer to buy southwestern territories, he instigated the Mexican War. The leadership of General Zachary Taylor and the U.S. Army's superior weaponry–one thousand Colt revolvers were issued to U.S. soldiers– led to the defeat of Mexico in 1848.

KEY EVENTS

1818 Polk graduates from the University of North Carolina.
1820 Polk begins to practice law.
1824 James K. Polk and Sarah Childress marry.
1825 Polk is elected to the U.S. House of

Representatives.
1835 Polk is named Speaker of the House of Representatives.
1839 Polk becomes governor of Tennessee.
1844 Polk is elected president.
1845 Polk appoints James

Buchanan secretary of state; the United States annexes Texas; Mexico severs diplomatic relations with the United States; the Polk administration establishes the U.S. Naval Academy.
1846 General Zachary Taylor's troops battle the

THE POLK PARTNERSHIP

James Polk pledged to expand the land held by the United States to the Pacific Ocean. He accomplished his goal with the support of the first lady, who served unofficially as his personal advisor. Perhaps because Sarah Polk had no children and few domestic responsibilities, she was able to work closely with her husband on many aspects of state business.

SARAH POLK

Sarah Polk took on a more independent role than was considered fitting for women of her era. The daughter of a rich Tennessee planter, she received a fine education but preferred politics to music and needlepoint. As first lady, she became known–and sometimes criticized–for her opinions. Having once said that if her husband were elected president she would "neither keep house nor make butter," Sarah was true to her word. She became James's advisor in private and read over his speeches. In public, however, she downplayed her role.

BIOGRAPHY

* ★ **YEARS AS FIRST LADY** 1845–1849
* ★ **BORN** Murfreesboro, Tenn., Sept. 4, 1803
* ★ **MARRIED** Murfreesboro, Tenn., Jan. 1, 1824
* ★ **DIED** Nashville, Tenn., Aug. 14, 1891, age 87

Sarah's inaugural fan with images of presidents

KEY EVENTS

Mexican army; Polk declares war on Mexico; the U.S. and Great Britain settle the boundary between Canada and the Oregon Territory; Polk signs the Walker Tariff Act, lowering taxes on imported goods.
1847 General Winfield Scott's troops capture Mexico City; Mexico is defeated.
1848 Gold is discovered in California; the U.S. and Mexico sign the Treaty of Guadalupe Hidalgo and the U.S. acquires California and New Mexico; Polk declines to run for a second term; General Zachary Taylor, hero of the Mexican War, is elected president.
1849 The Polks retire to their Tennessee home; James K. Polk dies.
1891 Sarah Polk dies.

TAYLOR

ZACHARY TAYLOR, a professional soldier, won the election of 1848 mainly because of his popularity as hero of the Mexican War. When he took office, the extension of slavery in the new territories was the pressing issue of the day. Taylor did not want the new territories to become slave states. He wanted to keep peace between the North, where slavery was regarded as an evil, and the South, which relied upon slave labor. Taylor threatened to veto the Compromise of 1850– legislation designed to resolve the issue–because he thought it favored the slave states. Fatefully, he died unexpectedly that year.

CALIFORNIA GOLD RUSH
Gold was discovered in California in 1848. In 1849, thousands of prospectors poured into the territory hoping to make their fortunes. This made the slavery question all the more pressing since California's population reached a level that enabled it to apply for statehood. Taylor wanted California to enter the United States as a free (nonslave) state.

BIOGRAPHY
★ 12TH PRESIDENT 1849–1850
★ BORN Montebello, Va., Nov. 24, 1784
★ INAUGURATED AS PRESIDENT Mar. 5, 1849
★ PARTY Whig
★ DIED Washington, D.C., July 9, 1850, age 65

KEY EVENTS

1808 Zachary Taylor becomes a U.S. army officer.
1810 Taylor and Margaret Smith marry.
1812 Taylor fights in the War of 1812.
1832 Taylor fights in the Black Hawk War in Illinois.

1836–7 Taylor fights in the Seminole War in Florida.
1846 Taylor's troops skirmish with Mexican forces; the Mexican War begins.
1847 Outnumbered by Mexican troops, Taylor wins an important victory at the Battle of Buena Vista;

Mexican War ends later this year.
1848 Taylor becomes both a general and a hero as a result of the Mexican War; gold is discovered in California; Taylor is elected president; immigration to the United States exceeds

MARGARET TAYLOR

After marrying Zachary Taylor in 1810, Margaret (who was nicknamed Peggy) spent the next fifteen years moving her family to remote military outposts throughout the United States. At one point, she became seriously ill; although she recovered, she was always treated as a semi-invalid. After the Mexican War ended, Peggy looked forward to retiring to their Louisiana home.

BIOGRAPHY
- ★ YEARS AS FIRST LADY 1849–1850
- ★ BORN Calvert County, Md., Sept. 21, 1788
- ★ DIED Pascagoula, Miss., Aug. 18, 1852, age 63

However, Zach's election to the presidency later that year disrupted her plans. Peggy was so uncomfortable with her role as first lady that their daughter, Betty Taylor Bliss, served as official hostess. While political cartoonists often depicted the first lady as a crude frontier woman, she was said to be gentle and refined.

Beaded bag belonging to Margaret Taylor

THE FIRST DAUGHTER

Margaret Taylor never sat for a photograph. Her daughter Betty Taylor Bliss was only twenty-three when she took on the duties of running the White House. A lieutenant colonel's wife, Betty had great poise and charm.

Betty Taylor Bliss

KEY EVENTS

100,000 for the year, an historical first.
1849 Betty Taylor Bliss, daughter of Margaret and Zachary, serves as the official White House hostess; the gold rush begins as thousands of prospectors arrive in California.

1850 The U.S. and Great Britain agree to joint control of any future canal built in Panama; members of Taylor's cabinet are involved in a financial scandal; Taylor dies unexpectedly of an intestinal disorder; Vice

President Millard Fillmore becomes president; after much debate, the Compromise of 1850 is passed by Congress; California enters the Union as a free state.
1852 Margaret Taylor dies.

FILLMORE

MILLARD FILLMORE grew up poor on a farm in New York State. In 1849, Fillmore became Zachary Taylor's vice president, and then president himself after Taylor's sudden death. Unlike Taylor, Fillmore favored the Compromise of 1850, which temporarily prevented the Union from breaking up. By signing the Fugitive Slave Act, though, Fillmore lost the support of the northerners in his Whig party and was not reelected.

BIOGRAPHY

★ 13TH PRESIDENT
 1850–1853
★ BORN Cayuga County, N.Y., Jan. 7, 1800
★ PARTY Whig
★ DIED Buffalo, N.Y., Mar. 8, 1874, age 74

BIOGRAPHY

★ YEARS AS FIRST LADY
 1850–1853
★ BORN Stillwater, N.Y., Mar. 13, 1798
★ DIED Washington, D.C., Mar. 30, 1853, age 55

ABIGAIL FILLMORE

Abigail was the first first lady to hold a paying job before her marriage: she was a teacher for almost seven years. She gave up her career after marrying Millard. By the time he became president in 1850, she had health problems. Although her daughter took over as hostess, Abigail made a lasting contribution by creating a library in the White House.

KEY EVENTS

1826 Millard Fillmore and Abigail Powers marry.
1848 Zachary Taylor is elected president with Fillmore as vice president.
1850 Fillmore becomes president after Zachary Taylor's death; the Compromise of 1850 is

passed; Fillmore demands enforcement of the Fugitive Slave Act, enraging many former supporters.
1852 Franklin Pierce defeats Millard Fillmore in the presidential election.
1853 Fillmore sends Commodore Matthew

Perry to Japan to establish trade links between the two nations; Abigail Fillmore dies.
1858 Millard Fillmore marries Caroline Carmichael McIntosh.
1874 Millard Fillmore dies.

PIERCE

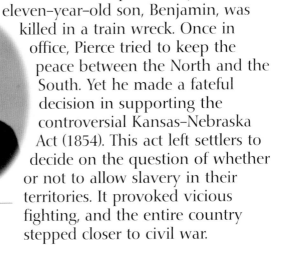

FRANKLIN PIERCE became president just after his eleven-year-old son, Benjamin, was killed in a train wreck. Once in office, Pierce tried to keep the peace between the North and the South. Yet he made a fateful decision in supporting the controversial Kansas–Nebraska Act (1854). This act left settlers to decide on the question of whether or not to allow slavery in their territories. It provoked vicious fighting, and the entire country stepped closer to civil war.

BIOGRAPHY

★ **14TH PRESIDENT** 1853–1857
★ **BORN** Hillsboro, N.H., Nov. 23, 1804
★ **PARTY** Democratic
★ **DIED** Concord, N.H., Oct. 8, 1869, age 64

BIOGRAPHY

★ **YEARS AS FIRST LADY** 1853–1857
★ **BORN** Hampton, N.H., Mar. 12, 1806
★ **DIED** Andover, Mass., Dec. 2, 1863, age 57

JANE PIERCE

After her older son died of typhoid fever in 1843, Jane Pierce clung to her younger boy, Benjamin, pictured with her here. His death sent her into deep mourning. She thought God had taken his life as punishment for Franklin's involvement in politics, which she thought to be "dirty."

KEY EVENTS

1834 Franklin Pierce and Jane Means Appleton marry.
1843 Franklin Pierce, Jr., dies of typhoid fever.
1852 Pierce is elected president.
1853 Pierce purchases land in present-day New Mexico and Arizona from Mexico.
1854 Congress passes the controversial Kansas-Nebraska Act, which allows residents of Kansas and Nebraska to decide whether to allow slavery; the Republican party is formed

in protest of the act.
1855 Fighting breaks out in Kansas over whether or not to allow slavery.
1856 James Buchanan is elected president.
1863 Jane Pierce dies.
1869 Franklin Pierce dies.

BUCHANAN

JAMES BUCHANAN entered the White House during a period of crisis, and his presidency was doomed from the start. For ten years the slavery debate had troubled the occupants of the White House, and Buchanan was no exception. A former lawyer from the North, he argued that slavery was legal under the Constitution and urged for compromise on the issue. But the abolitionist movement was growing in strength. In both the North and the South, trust and reason were giving way to fear and anger. Buchanan became a spectator as events spun out of control. By the time he left office, civil war was inevitable.

BIOGRAPHY

★ 15TH PRESIDENT 1857–1861
★ PARTY Democratic
★ BORN Cove Gap, Penn., Apr. 23, 1791
★ DIED Lancaster, Penn., June 1, 1868, age 77

JOHN BROWN'S RAID

In 1859, John Brown, a radical abolitionist, attempted to start a slave rebellion. His aim was to capture the federal arsenal at Harpers Ferry, Virginia. His plan failed, and Brown was captured and hanged. Yet John Brown's legend lived on, in poetry and song, and struck fear in the hearts of many southerners.

KEY EVENTS

1834 James Buchanan is elected to U.S. Senate.
1845 Polk appoints Buchanan secretary of state.
1856 Buchanan is elected president.
1857 Dred Scott, a slave, sues his owner for his freedom, arguing that he had lived in a free state and this made him free; the Supreme Court rules that Scott is not a citizen and therefore cannot file a lawsuit; abolitionist cause is dealt a major blow with this decision.
1858 The proslavery constitution of Kansas is voted out; controversy ensues over whether Kansas should be admitted as a free or slave state.
1859 John Brown's raid

FREDERICK DOUGLASS

A former slave, Frederick Douglass was the foremost black abolitionist of his time. He was a brilliant orator and ran his own antislavery newspaper, the *North Star*. After John Brown's raid, President Buchanan sent federal troops to arrest Douglass. Douglass fled the country, but returned soon after to continue his fight.

Harriet Lane

Harriet Lane was raised by her uncle James Buchanan, who was the first bachelor to become president. When he took office in 1857, twenty–six–year–old Harriet served as his official hostess. She brought glitter and glamour to an administration marked by growing hostility between northern and southern states over the issue of slavery. After the Civil War, Harriet married Henry Elliot Johnston, a wealthy banker. Widowed eighteen years later, she devoted herself to worthy causes and donated her fine art collection–now at the Smithsonian Institution–to the nation.

BIOGRAPHY

★ YEARS AS FIRST LADY
1857–1861
★ BORN Mercersburg, Penn.,
May 9, 1830
★ DIED Rhode Island,
July 3, 1903, age 73

KEY EVENTS

occurs; the plan fails and he is captured and hanged.
1860 Abraham Lincoln is elected president; South Carolina secedes from the Union.
1861 Kansas is

admitted to the Union as a free state; other southern states follow South Carolina's lead and the Confederate States of America is formed; Buchanan cannot resolve the crisis; Lincoln enters the White

House; the Civil War begins.
1866 Harriet Lane marries banker Henry Elliot Johnston.
1868 James Buchanan dies.
1903 Harriet Lane Johnston dies.

LINCOLN

ABRAHAM LINCOLN grew up in a log cabin on the frontier. He became a lawyer and a politician, and believed in liberty for all Americans. He especially deplored slavery and spoke out against its expansion. In 1860, Lincoln was elected president. The southern states viewed him as a threat and left the Union. Lincoln faced a country on the brink of civil war. He had to bind the nation together again, a task that no other president has had to undertake.

Newspaper announcing secession of southern states

THE UNION COLLAPSES

Rather than accept Lincoln as president, most southern states chose to secede, or separate, from the Union in 1861. Lincoln did not believe the southern states had a constitutional right to secede. He had sworn to uphold the laws of the land and was determined to reunite the country, even if it meant fighting a civil war.

BIOGRAPHY
★ 16TH PRESIDENT 1861–1865
★ BORN Hardin County, Ky., Feb. 12, 1809
★ INAUGURATED AS PRESIDENT First term: Mar. 4, 1861 Second term: Mar. 4, 1865
★ PARTY Republican
★ DIED Washington, D.C., Apr. 15, 1865, age 56

KEY EVENTS

1834 Abraham Lincoln is elected to the Illinois state legislature.
1836 Abraham Lincoln begins to practice law.
1842 Abraham Lincoln and Mary Todd marry.
1846 Lincoln is elected to U.S. House of Representatives.
1856 Lincoln joins the Republican party.
1858 Lincoln loses the U.S. Senate race to Stephen Douglas.
1860 The Republican party names Lincoln its presidential candidate; he wins the election with less than 40 percent of the vote.
1861 Eleven southern states secede from the Union and form the Confederate States of America; Jefferson Davis, a former U.S.

MARY LINCOLN

Mary Lincoln had the misfortune to enter the White House as civil war divided the nation. Well-meaning and intelligent, her southern birth led northerners to suspect her of being a spy and southerners to condemn her Union sympathies. Mary believed that slavery was wrong, but her efforts to speak out against it were misunderstood. Devoted to her husband and her position, she retreated briefly from public life when her eleven-year-old son Willie died in 1862. After Lincoln was assassinated in 1865, she was again plunged into grief, from which she never fully recovered.

BIOGRAPHY

★ **YEARS AS FIRST LADY** 1861–1865
★ **BORN** Lexington, Ky., Dec. 13, 1818
★ **MARRIED** Springfield, Ill., Nov. 4, 1842
★ **CHILDREN** Robert Todd, Edward Baker, William Wallace, Thomas
★ **DIED** Springfield, Ill., July 16, 1882, age 63

WOMEN AND THE WAR BETWEEN THE STATES

Women's lives were dramatically affected by the conflict. With the men off to war, both northern and southern women took over important tasks outside the home. Many nursed the sick; others raised money for the war effort while managing farms or plantations. Mary Lincoln visited the suffering and supported the abolitionist, or antislavery, movement. Many women who joined abolitionist groups realized they had something in common with those in bondage. They too were denied many basic rights, such as the right to vote.

KEY EVENTS

congressman, senator, and secretary of war, is elected president of the Confederacy; the U.S. Civil War breaks out when Confederate troops fire on Fort Sumter; the Union army is defeated at the first battle at Bull Run; the Union navy begins a blockade of southern ports. **1862** Eleven-year-old Willie Lincoln dies; the Confederates are stopped at Antietam; the Union army is defeated at Fredericksburg; Congress passes the Homestead Act, giving 160 acres of public land to settlers who work the land for five years. **1863** Lincoln issues his Emancipation Proclamation, freeing all slaves in areas of rebellion.

THE CIVIL WAR

On April 12, 1861, Confederates fired on Fort Sumter, a Union stronghold in Charleston harbor, South Carolina. This attack was the beginning to the bloodiest conflict in American history. The vicious fighting of the Civil War lasted four agonizing years. Lincoln was deeply pained by the bloodshed, but he never lost faith in his cause. With the Emancipation Proclamation, signed in 1863, Lincoln freed slaves in the Confederate states. Slaves were considered Confederate property, and as commander-in-chief of the Union forces, Lincoln was entitled to order the seizure of enemy property. He had no constitutional right, however, to order the freeing of slaves in the North. Nevertheless, African-Americans throughout the country rejoiced. Under his firm leadership, the Union eventually prevailed with Confederate general Robert E. Lee's surrender on April 9, 1865.

George McClellan   *Abraham Lincoln*   *George A. Custer*

Lincoln and McClellan meet at Antietam, 1862

KEY EVENTS

1863 Congress passes the Conscription Act to draft soldiers for the Union army; West Virginia becomes a state after seceding from Virginia and siding with the Union; the Confederates are defeated at Gettysburg.

1863 Union General Ulysses S. Grant wins at Vicksburg; riots erupt in New York City in protest of the military draft; Lincoln gives the Gettysburg Address to dedicate a new Union cemetery on the site of

the deadliest battle of the war; Lincoln announces his "Ten-Percent Plan," for Reconstruction, or rebuilding the Union.
1864 Lincoln appoints General Ulysses S. Grant commander of Union army; Union general

LINCOLN IS ASSASSINATED

Five days after Lee's surrender, John Wilkes Booth, a Confederate sympathizer, shot and killed President Lincoln as he watched a play at Ford's Theater in Washington, D.C. The assassination of Abraham Lincoln stunned and saddened the nation. The nation had lost a

great leader when he was still badly needed. Lincoln had not believed in punishing the South for the war. With him gone, those bent on revenge were able to gain influence.

ON THE BATTLEFIELD

The Civil War was one of America's bitterest conflicts. Soldiers on both sides fought fiercely for their cause. Because of the introduction of effective new weapons, losses were heavy. In 1863, at the Battle of Gettysburg alone, over 50,000 men were lost. In all, some 600,000 soldiers–two percent of the population–died in the war.

Union uniform cap, called a kepi

KEY EVENTS

William T. Sherman captures Atlanta; Lincoln is reelected president; Sherman leads his troops in a "March to the Sea" across Georgia, leaving devastation in their wake. **1865** Congress passes the Thirteenth Amendment, abolishing slavery, and sends it to the states for ratification; Freedman's Bureau is created to assist former slaves; General Robert E. Lee, commander of the Confederate army, surrenders to Grant at Appomattox, Virginia; the Civil War ends; Lincoln is assassinated by John Wilkes Booth; Vice President Andrew Johnson enters the White House. **1882** Mary Todd Lincoln dies.

JOHNSON

ANDREW JOHNSON, a Democrat from Tennessee, was the only United States senator from the South to remain loyal to the Union at the start of the Civil War. For his steadfastness, Johnson was nominated vice president in 1864. In April, 1865, after Lincoln was assassinated, Johnson became president. In 1868, Congress tried to impeach Johnson because he opposed harsh Congressional policies toward the defeated South. Although Johnson was spared removal from office by one vote, his presidency was all but over.

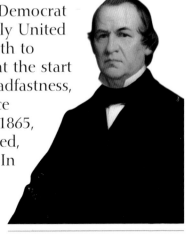

BIOGRAPHY

★ 17TH PRESIDENT 1865–1869
★ BORN Raleigh, N.C., Dec. 29, 1808
★ INAUGURATED AS PRESIDENT April 15, 1865
★ PARTY Democratic
★ DIED Carter County, Tenn., July 31, 1875, age 66

Vest made by Johnson

THE TENNESSEE TAILOR

Johnson was nicknamed the "Tennessee Tailor" because he began his working life as a tailor's apprentice. He received no formal schooling and his wife, Eliza, taught him how to read and write. By the age of 33, Johnson was elected to Congress.

KEY EVENTS

1827 Andrew Johnson and Eliza McCardle marry.
1842 Johnson is elected to U.S. House of Representatives.
1852 Johnson is elected governor of Tennessee.
1856 Johnson is elected to U.S. Senate.

1861 The Civil War begins; Johnson is the only southern senator to reject the Confederacy and remain in Congress.
1864 Johnson is elected vice president.
1865 Lincoln is assassinated and Johnson

becomes president; the Thirteenth Amendment, freeing all slaves, is ratified; Congress creates a committee to investigate Johnson's Reconstruction policies.
1866 Congress overrides Johnson's veto and passes

THE PRESIDENT IS IMPEACHED

In 1868, Andrew Johnson became the first president in history to be impeached, or put on trial, by the Senate. There were no constitutional grounds for prosecuting Johnson, just political disagreements over his postwar Reconstruction policies. As president, Johnson tried to enact Lincoln's policy of leniency toward the defeated southern states. But a group of congressmen called the Radical Republicans resented giving too much power back to the former Confederates. When Johnson refused to yield to their demands, the Radicals in Congress impeached him.

Impeachment ticket

ELIZA JOHNSON

An invalid when her husband took office, Eliza Johnson rarely left her room in the White House. Still, Eliza contributed a great deal to her husband's career, beginning with teaching Andrew to read and write after they were married. Later, as he became active in politics, Eliza raised their five children. However, Eliza was a reluctant first lady, and their daughter Martha Johnson Patterson acted as hostess for her father. Mrs. Patterson was an unassuming woman who remained gracious toward visitors even during her father's impeachment trial.

BIOGRAPHY

★ **YEARS AS FIRST LADY** 1865–1869
★ **BORN** Leesburg, Tenn., Oct. 4, 1810
★ **MARRIED** Greeneville, Tenn., Dec. 17, 1827
★ **CHILDREN** Martha, Charles, Mary, Robert, Andrew
★ **DIED** Greene County, Tenn., Jan. 15, 1876, age 65

KEY EVENTS

the Civil Rights Act of 1866, which protects the rights of former slaves; Congress overrides Johnson's veto and passes the Fourteenth Amendment, extending citizenship to all people born in the United States.
1867 Congress passes the

Military Reconstruction Act, establishing military rule in the former Confederate states.
1868 Johnson is impeached, or put on trial for improper conduct, by the Radical Republicans in Congress; Johnson is not

convicted so he remains in office; Ulysses S. Grant is elected president.
1874 Johnson is reelected to U.S. Senate.
1875 Andrew Johnson dies.
1876 Eliza McCardle Johnson dies.

GRANT

ULYSSES S. GRANT became a national hero as the leading Union general. Three years after the end of the Civil War, he won the presidency in 1868. Unfortunately, Grant proved to be ill-suited to the White House. He had no experience in politics and no real desire to use the full powers of his high office. Unwittingly, he let dishonest people take advantage of him. Scandals discredited his administration. After eight years, Grant was happy to leave the White House.

BIOGRAPHY

★ 18TH PRESIDENT
1869–1877
★ BORN Point Pleasant, Ohio, Apr. 27, 1822
★ INAUGURATED AS PRESIDENT First term: Mar. 4, 1869 Second term: Mar. 4, 1873
★ PARTY Republican
★ DIED Mount McGregor, N.Y., July 23, 1885, age 63

GENERAL GRANT

Grant had been frustrated in several occupations–soldier, farmer, realtor, store clerk–before becoming a Union general. On the battlefield, Grant soon proved himself to be a military dynamo.

Grant with horse during Civil War

KEY EVENTS

1839 Ulysses S. Grant enters West Point.
1848 The Mexican War ends with Grant as hero; Grant and Julia Dent marry.
1864 Grant becomes Union commander-in-chief during the Civil War.

1865 The Civil War ends; Reconstruction begins.
1868 Grant is elected president.
1870 The Fifteenth Amendment, granting African-American men the right to vote, is ratified; Congress passes legislation

to protect the rights of former slaves.
1872 Railroad scandals taint Grant's administration; Grant is reelected president.
1873 An economic depression strikes the nation; the president's

SOLDIERING ON

During his retirement, Grant continued to experience bad luck. In 1884, he lost his entire savings to an unscrupulous investment broker, and, a short time later, he was diagnosed with throat cancer. Grant decided to write his memoirs in order to provide for his family. He finished just one week before he died. His *Personal Memoirs* became an instant best-seller.

JULIA GRANT

Julia Dent preferred fishing and horseback riding to books. Such spirit appealed to Lieutenant Ulysses S. Grant–he fell in love with her at first sight. They married in 1848, and had four children. General Grant's military leadership during the Civil War enabled the couple to enter the White House on a wave of popularity. Julia was a well-liked first lady known for her direct and unpretentious manner. With the Union restored, Americans did not criticize the first lady for her lavish dinner parties or expensive purchases as they had Mary Lincoln, prompting Mrs. Grant to look back on her White House years as "quite the happiest period of my life."

BIOGRAPHY

★ **YEARS AS FIRST LADY** 1869–1877
★ **BORN** St. Louis, Mo., Jan. 26, 1826
★ **MARRIED** St. Louis, Mo., Aug. 22, 1848
★ **CHILDREN** Frederick Dent, Ulysses Simpson, Ellen Wrenshall, Jesse Root
★ **DIED** Washington D.C., Dec. 14, 1902, age 76

KEY EVENTS

salary is raised from $25,000 to $50,000 a year. **1874** After the congressional elections, the Democratic party regains control of the House of Representatives. **1875** Threats and violence bring the Democratic party back into power in Mississippi and other southern states. **1876** The presidential election between Rutherford B. Hayes and Samuel Tilden is disputed, with no clear winner. **1877** A Congressional committee votes and Hayes is elected president after a compromise is worked out. **1884** Grant loses his life savings. **1885** Ulysses S. Grant dies. **1902** Julia Grant dies.

HAYES

RUTHERFORD B. HAYES had been a Union general during the Civil War, like Ulysses S. Grant. In 1877, he won a controversial election by one vote. Congress decided the contest, which left many of Hayes's opponents feeling cheated. They referred to Hayes as "His Fraudulency" and "Rutherfraud" B. Hayes. Hayes proved to be an even-handed but unexceptional president. He was lenient with the southern states and removed the last remaining federal troops from their midst. He also used federal troops to move Indians onto reservations. By the end of his presidency, during which industry and business boomed in the United States, Hayes had managed to win over his critics.

A POLITICAL BARGAIN

Hayes's opponent in the 1876 election was Democrat Samuel J. Tilden. When Tilden lost the election, southern Democrats were so outraged that they threatened to secede. They declared that they would only accept Hayes as president if he agreed to remove federal troops from the South. Hayes agreed.

Hayes campaign banner

BIOGRAPHY

★ **19TH PRESIDENT**
1877–1881
★ **BORN** Delaware, Ohio, Oct. 4, 1822
★ **PARTY** Republican
★ **DIED** Fremont, Oh., Jan. 17 1893, age 71

KEY EVENTS

1843 Rutherford B. Hayes graduates from Kenyon College.
1845 Hayes receives a law degree from Harvard University.
1850 Lucy Webb graduates from Wesleyan Female College.

1852 Rutherford B. Hayes and Lucy Webb marry.
1856 Hayes helps found the Ohio Republican party.
1864 Hayes is elected to U.S. House of Representatives.
1868 Hayes is elected governor of Ohio.

1876 General Custer is defeated in the Battle of Little Big Horn.
1877 After a close presidential race, a special commission declares Hayes the winner; Hayes withdraws federal troops from the former

THE BATTLE OF LITTLE BIG HORN

In the 1870s, gold was discovered in the Black Hills of South Dakota. The U.S. government tried to the move the Sioux and Cheyenne who lived there onto reservations. On June 25, 1876, a federal cavalry, led by George A. Custer, attacked the camp of Chief Sitting Bull on the Little Big Horn River in Montana. Custer and all his men were killed in the battle, but the Indian victory was a short one. Federal troops descended on the area and forced them to surrender.

LUCY HAYES

Lucy Hayes was the first college graduate to hold the position of first lady. She was also a woman of strong religious and moral beliefs. A supporter of a nineteenth-century movement against alcohol and drugs known as temperance, Mrs. Hayes, with her husband's approval, refused to serve liquor in the White House. Her ban earned her the memorable nickname Lemonade Lucy. A devoted wife and mother, Mrs. Hayes declined to act as spokesperson for women's rights groups, who had hoped the educated first lady would become their ally.

BIOGRAPHY

★ **YEARS AS FIRST LADY** 1877–1881
★ **BORN** Chillicothe, Ohio, Aug. 28, 1831
★ **MARRIED** Cincinnati, Ohio, Dec. 30, 1852
★ **CHILDREN** Richard Austin, Webb Cook, Rutherford Platt, Joseph Thompson, George Crook, Fanny, Scott Russell, Manning Force
★ **DIED** Freemont, Ohio, June 25, 1889, age 57

KEY EVENTS

Confederate states and Reconstruction is over; Hayes sends in federal troops to end a national railroad strike.
1878 Lucy Hayes hosts the first Easter egg roll at the White House; Congress overrides Hayes's veto of the Bland-Allison Act, which provided for federal purchase of silver to be coined into silver dollars.
1879 Hayes signs an act allowing female lawyers to practice before the Supreme Court.
1880 Hayes declines to run for a second term; James A. Garfield is elected president.
1881 Rutherford and Lucy Hayes retire to their home in Ohio.
1889 Lucy Hayes dies.
1893 Rutherford B. Hayes dies.

GARFIELD

JAMES A. GARFIELD rose from poverty to become a lawyer, Civil War hero, and successful politician. He was the third Civil War general to become president, but the battlefield proved to be a safer place than the president's office. Four months into his term, an assassin shot Garfield. As president, he had wanted to reform the civil service system and the post office. Unfortunately, tragedy intervened and he became the second president to be assassinated.

BIOGRAPHY

★ **20TH PRESIDENT** 1881
★ **BORN** Orange Township, Ohio, Nov. 19, 1831
★ **PARTY** Republican
★ **DIED** Elberon, N.J., Sept. 19, 1881, age 49

LUCRETIA GARFIELD

Lucretia, known as Crete, wrote diaries that show her to be a wise and independent woman who acted as advisor to James. After he was shot, she nursed him until his death.

BIOGRAPHY

★ **YEARS AS FIRST LADY** 1881
★ **BORN** Hiram, Ohio, Apr. 19, 1832
★ **MARRIED** Hiram, Ohio, Nov. 11, 1858
★ **CHILDREN** Eliza Arabella, Harry Augustus, James Rudolph, Mary, Irvin McDowell, Abram, Edward
★ **DIED** Pasadena, Calif., Mar. 14, 1918, age 85

KEY EVENTS

1858 James A. Garfield and Lucretia Rudolph marry; Garfield is elected to the Ohio state legislature.
1862 Garfield is elected to U.S. House of Representatives.
1880 Garfield is elected president.
1881 Ill with malaria, Lucretia Garfield leaves Washington to recuperate; after only four months in office, Garfield is shot by Charles Guiteau; Garfield survives for more than two months after being shot, and his wife returns to nurse him; Garfield dies of blood poisoning on September 19; Chester A. Arthur becomes president.
1918 Lucretia Garfield dies.

ARTHUR

CHESTER A. ARTHUR became president when Garfield was assassinated. For years, he had been a "spoilsman," which meant he had been given political jobs in return for his loyalty to the Republican party. As president, Arthur's attitude changed. He now believed that politicians should earn federal jobs based on their merits. He signed legislation requiring federal job seekers to pass exams before entering the civil service. He was not nominated for a second term.

BIOGRAPHY
★ 21ST PRESIDENT
  1881–1885
★ **BORN** North Fairfield, Vt.,
  Oct. 5, 1830
★ **PARTY** Republican
★ **DIED** New York, N.Y.,
  Nov. 18, 1886, age 56

BIOGRAPHY
★ NEVER SERVED
  AS FIRST LADY
★ **BORN** Fredericksburg,
  Va., Aug. 30, 1837
★ **MARRIED** New York,
  N.Y., Oct. 29, 1859
★ **CHILDREN** William
  Lewis Herndon,
  Chester Alan, Ellen
★ **DIED** New York, N.Y.,
  Jan. 12, 1880, age 42

ELLEN ARTHUR
Ellen Herndon was an accomplished singer who met and married Chester Arthur in New York City. Just as his political career was taking off, Ellen died suddenly of pneumonia. When Arthur became president, his sister Mary Arthur McElroy served as official hostess.

KEY EVENTS

1859 Chester Arthur and Ellen Herndon marry.
1871 Arthur is appointed customs collector for the port of New York.
1880 Ellen Arthur dies; Arthur is elected vice president.
1881 Upon Garfield's death, Arthur becomes president.
1882 Congress passes the Chinese Exclusion Act, which prevents Chinese immigration to the United States for ten years; U.S. Navy opens trade with Korea.
1883 Arthur signs the Pendleton Act, a civil service reform bill; the United States acquires a naval station at Pearl Harbor in the Hawaiian Islands.
1886 Chester Arthur dies.

CLEVELAND

GROVER CLEVELAND was the only president to serve two nonconsecutive terms. He was ousted from office in 1889 by Benjamin Harrison, but returned to the White House four years later. Cleveland believed in "hands–off" government and vetoed more legislation than any president before him, earning the nickname "Old Veto." An economic depression plagued his second term. He did not believe the federal government should intervene. When the economy did not recover, Cleveland used federal troops to suppress labor unrest.

BIOGRAPHY

★ **22ND PRESIDENT** 1885–1889
★ **24TH PRESIDENT** 1893–1897
★ **BORN** Caldwell, N.J., Mar. 18, 1837
★ **PARTY** Democratic
★ **DIED** Princeton, N.J., June 24, 1908, age 71

Cleveland campaign banner

THE PULLMAN RAILROAD STRIKE

In 1894, Cleveland sent federal troops to break up a strike by railroad workers at the Pullman Palace Car Company in Chicago. The strike, the result of a pay cut, was interfering with the delivery of the mail. He had the strike leader arrested, and the workers were forced to accept lower wages.

KEY EVENTS

1882 Grover Cleveland serves as mayor of Buffalo, N.Y.; Cleveland is elected governor of New York.
1884 Cleveland is elected president.
1886 Cleveland and Frances Folsom get married in the White House; Frances is the youngest first lady in U.S. history; the Statue of Liberty is dedicated.
1887 Congress passes the Interstate Commerce Act, regulating railroads and other ground transportation.
1888 Benjamin Harrison defeats Cleveland in the presidential election; Cleveland goes to work for a New York City law firm.
1892 Cleveland is reelected president, defeating Harrison.
1893 The United States suffers from a severe

FRANCES CLEVELAND

He called her Frank, and she called him Uncle Cleve. She was a twenty-one-year-old beauty, and he was a forty-eight-year-old bachelor. They were married in the White House, which was the first wedding of a president to take place in the mansion. When Frances Folsom wed Grover Cleveland, the press pursued the couple relentlessly. As first lady, she became a popular object of devotion. Some historians think that her popularity helped Cleveland get reelected.

BIOGRAPHY

★ **YEARS AS FIRST LADY** 1886–1889 and 1893–1897
★ **BORN** Buffalo, N.Y., July 21, 1864
★ **MARRIED** White House, Washington D.C., June 2, 1886
★ **CHILDREN** Ruth, Esther, Marion, Richard Folsom, Francis Grover
★ **DIED** Baltimore, Md., Oct. 29, 1947, age 83

THE QUEEN OF DIAMONDS

The image of Mrs. Cleveland appeared everywhere, even on such objects as playing cards. The president became incensed by the threat to his family's privacy. He tried to stop Frances's likeness from being used in advertising. Ironically, Cleveland supported a bill concerning the commercial use of celebrities' names and images without their written consent–it did not pass.

Campaign plate featuring Frances Cleveland

KEY EVENTS

economic depression; the Clevelands' daughter Esther is the first child of a president born in the White House.
1894 Cleveland sends federal troops to break up a strike at the Pullman Palace Car Company in Chicago; workers are forced to accept lower wages.
1896 The Democratic party does not nominate Cleveland for a third term; William McKinley is elected president.
1897 Grover and Francis Cleveland retire to Princeton, New Jersey.
1908 Grover Cleveland dies.
1913 Frances Cleveland marries archaeologist Thomas Jex Preston.
1947 Frances Cleveland dies.

HARRISON

BENJAMIN HARRISON came from a distinguished political family: his grandfather, William Henry Harrison, was the ninth president. Harrison supported the Sherman Antitrust Act of 1890, which regulated big business. At the same time, though, Harrison signed the McKinley Tariff Act, which protected big business from foreign competition. In foreign affairs, Harrison strengthened the navy to expand U.S. influence in Central America and the Pacific.

BIOGRAPHY

★ **23RD PRESIDENT** 1889–1893
★ **BORN** North Bend, Ohio, Aug. 20, 1833
★ **PARTY** Republican
★ **DIED** Indianapolis, Ind., Mar. 13, 1901, age 67

CAROLINE HARRISON

Caroline Harrison distinguished herself as a volunteer for the sick and the orphaned and used her influence as first lady to advance worthy causes. She died in the White House in 1892, leaving her daughter, Mary McKee, to act as hostess.

BIOGRAPHY

★ **YEARS AS FIRST LADY** 1889–1892
★ **BORN** Oxford, Ohio, Oct. 1, 1832
★ **MARRIED** Oxford, Ohio, Oct. 20, 1853
★ **CHILDREN** Russell Benjamin, Mary Scott
★ **DIED** Washington, D.C., Oct. 25, 1892, age 60

KEY EVENTS

1849 Caroline Scott graduates from the Oxford Female Institute.
1853 Benjamin Harrison and Caroline Scott marry.
1880 Harrison is elected to U.S. Senate.
1888 Harrison is elected president.

1890 Harrison signs the Sherman Antitrust Act, allowing the federal government to regulate private businesses and prosecute illegal monopolies; Harrison signs the McKinley Tariff Act.
1892 Caroline Harrison

dies; daughter Mary Harrison McKee takes over as official White House hostess; Grover Cleveland defeats Harrison in the presidential election.
1901 Benjamin Harrison dies.

McKINLEY

WILLIAM MCKINLEY is best remembered for his foreign policy successes. In 1898, he helped the Cubans win their independence from Spain. Once the Spanish were defeated, the United States acquired Guam, Puerto Rico, and the Philippine Islands. Under McKinley, the nation became a global power. On September 6, 1901, an anarchist–a person who opposes any sort of government–shot McKinley. Eight days later, the president died from his gunshot wounds.

BIOGRAPHY

★ **25TH PRESIDENT** 1897–1901
★ **BORN** Niles, Ohio, Jan. 29, 1843
★ **PARTY** Republican
★ **DIED** Buffalo, N.Y., Sept. 14, 1901, age 58

IDA MCKINLEY
The intelligent and beautiful Ida Saxton became an invalid after the deaths of her mother and her infant daughter. Her condition made public appearances awkward, but she continued to act as first lady until her husband's death.

BIOGRAPHY

★ **YEARS AS FIRST LADY** 1897–1901
★ **BORN** Canton, Ohio, June 8, 1847
★ **MARRIED** Canton, Ohio, Jan. 25, 1871
★ **CHILDREN** Katherine, Ida
★ **DIED** Canton, Ohio, May 26, 1907, age 59

KEY EVENTS

1871 William McKinley and Ida Saxton marry.
1873 Ida McKinley suffers a nervous breakdown, followed by epileptic seizures.
1892 McKinley becomes governor of Ohio.
1896 McKinley is elected

president.
1897 McKinley signs the Dingley Tariff, raising taxes on imported goods.
1898 Spanish-American War begins; the U.S. acquires Guam, Puerto Rico, and the Philippine Islands from Spain; Hawaii

is annexed.
1901 McKinley is shot and killed by an anarchist; Ida McKinley's epileptic seizures cease; Vice President Theodore Roosevelt assumes the presidency.
1907 Ida McKinley dies.

ROOSEVELT

THEODORE ROOSEVELT

became president after McKinley's 1901 assassination. Roosevelt was well qualified for the job. Previously a writer and a cowboy, he had also held important political posts and was full of energy and idealism. During the Spanish–American War, he led a volunteer cavalry unit known as the Rough Riders. As president, Roosevelt wanted all Americans to have a "square deal," and he set about redressing the balance between rich business interests and the needs of workers.

TEDDY'S BEAR

Roosevelt was once a sickly boy plagued by asthma. Yet he became a lifelong believer in strenuous exercise and was an avid hunter. On a hunting trip in 1902, Roosevelt refused to shoot a captured black bear. A cartoon appeared in the *Washington Post* about the incident. A toy maker named a stuffed bear "Teddy" after the president. Soon "Teddy's bears" were being sold as toys across the nation.

BIOGRAPHY

★ **26TH PRESIDENT** 1901–1909
★ **BORN** New York, N.Y., Oct. 27, 1858
★ **INAUGURATED AS PRESIDENT** First term: Sept. 14, 1901 Second term: Mar. 4, 1905
★ **PARTY** Republican
★ **CHILDREN** (with first wife, Alice Hathaway Lee) Alice Lee; (with second wife, Edith Carow) Theodore Jr., Kermit, Ethel Carow, Archibald Bulloch, Quentin
★ **DIED** Oyster Bay, N.Y., Jan. 6, 1919, age 60

KEY EVENTS

1880 Theodore Roosevelt graduates from Harvard University; Roosevelt marries Alice Hathaway Lee.
1882 Roosevelt is elected to the New York State legislature.
1884 Alice Roosevelt dies.

1886 Roosevelt marries Edith Kermit Carow.
1898 Spanish-American War begins; Roosevelt resigns as assistant secretary of the navy to organize a cavalry unit and fight in the war; returning from the war a hero,

Roosevelt is elected governor of New York State.
1900 McKinley is reelected president with Roosevelt as vice president.
1901 McKinley is assassinated; Roosevelt

THE WHITE HOUSE GANG

The Roosevelt children often caused mayhem at the White House. The younger sons were nicknamed the White House Gang. They had a menagerie of pets and slid down the central staircase on metal trays.

Roosevelt's popular elder daughter Alice enjoyed scandalizing the public. Her father reportedly said: "I can be President of the United States or I can control Alice. I cannot possibly do both."

EDITH ROOSEVELT

Edith Kermit Carow and Teddy Roosevelt were childhood playmates, but it was not until he was a widower with a young daughter that they were married. As first lady, Edith presided over a complete restoration of the White House, and added the West Wing for presidential offices. She also created a picture gallery of first ladies in the White House. Given the public's fascination with her children's antics, Mrs. Roosevelt became the first first lady to hire a social secretary to help control the first family's image.

BIOGRAPHY

★ **YEARS AS FIRST LADY** 1901–1909
★ **BORN** Norwich, Ct., Aug. 6, 1861
★ **MARRIED** London, England, Dec. 2, 1886
★ **DIED** Oyster Bay, N.Y., Sept. 30, 1948, age 87

The Roosevelt family (from left to right): Quentin, Theodore, Theodore, Jr., Archibald, Alice, Kermit, Edith, Ethel

KEY EVENTS

becomes president; Booker T. Washington, renowned African-American educator and leader, dines at the White House; he is the first African-American invited to dinner at the White House.

1902 Roosevelt begins trust-busting, or prosecuting monopolies in the business world; Roosevelt intervenes in a coal miners' strike and wins higher wages and a shorter workday for workers; Roosevelt refuses to shoot a captured black bear on a hunting trip; the story makes the news; "Teddy's bears" begin to be sold as toys.

1903 Roosevelt establishes the first federal wildlife refuge.

1904 Roosevelt is elected president.

PROTECTION FOR THE WORKERS

Roosevelt was an idealistic president who believed that ordinary Americans should be protected against the power of industrialists. When coal miners in Pennsylvania went on strike for higher wages in 1902, Roosevelt threatened to seize the mines unless the owners agreed to arbitration. He invited both sides to Washington to discuss their differences. The miners proceeded to win many of their demands.

Roosevelt banner

THE GREAT OUTDOORS MAN

Roosevelt had a passion for the outdoors and created four of the first federal game reserves. A farsighted environmentalist, Roosevelt believed that American land and animals were resources not to be squandered but maintained properly. By executive order, he preserved millions of acres of national forest and established five national parks.

Roosevelt's leather cowboy chaps

KEY EVENTS

1904 Roosevelt appoints William H. Taft secretary of war; construction begins on the Panama Canal.

1905 Roosevelt creates the Forest Service to manage national forests; Roosevelt helps mediate the end to a war between Russia and Japan.

1906 Congress passes the Pure Food and Drug Act to regulate the quality of food sold to American citizens.

1908 Taft is elected president.

1912 Roosevelt forms the Progressive, or "Bull Moose" party; he runs for president and is defeated.

1914 The Panama Canal is completed.

1919 Teddy Roosevelt dies.

1948 Edith Roosevelt dies.

TAFT

WILLIAM H. TAFT continued Roosevelt's progressive policies and initiated more antitrust suits than did Roosevelt. Taft's administration also supported the adoption of the Sixteenth Amendment, which allowed for the collection of personal income taxes. After leaving the White House, Taft served as chief justice of the Supreme Court from 1921 to 1930, making him the only president to hold this post.

BIOGRAPHY

★ **27TH PRESIDENT** 1909–1913
★ **BORN** Cincinnati, Ohio, Sept. 15, 1857
★ **INAUGURATED AS PRESIDENT** March 4, 1909
★ **PARTY** Republican
★ **DIED** Washington D.C., Mar. 8, 1930, age 72

HELEN TAFT

Helen Herron formed a salon, or intellectual group, at the age of twenty-two and asked attorney William Taft to join. After they married, she played an important role in her husband's political career. Just two months into his presidency, Helen suffered a stroke. Still, she managed to put her own stamp on the White House.

BIOGRAPHY

★ **YEARS AS FIRST LADY** 1909–1913
★ **BORN** Cincinnati, Ohio, June 2, 1861
★ **MARRIED** Cincinnati, Ohio, June 19, 1886
★ **CHILDREN** Robert Alphonso, Helen, Charles Phelps II
★ **DIED** Washington, D.C., May 22, 1943, age 82

KEY EVENTS

1878 William H. Taft graduates from Yale University.
1886 William Taft and Helen Herron marry.
1892 Taft is appointed a federal court judge.
1904 President Roosevelt appoints Taft secretary of war.
1908 Taft is elected president.
1910 Congress passes the Mann Act to stop prostitution.
1912 Woodrow Wilson defeats Taft in the presidential election.
1913 The Sixteenth Amendment, establishing the collection of personal income taxes, is passed.
1921 Taft is appointed chief justice of the Supreme Court.
1930 William Taft dies.
1943 Helen Taft dies.

WILSON

WOODROW WILSON

was a dynamic reformer in domestic affairs, signing legislation to lower tariffs and to regulate businesses and banks. In foreign matters, he tried to keep his country out of World War I, but when American involvement became inevitable, he worked hard for peace. At the end of the war, Wilson helped negotiate the Treaty of Versailles, but he was bitterly disappointed when the Senate rejected it.

BIOGRAPHY

★ **28TH PRESIDENT** 1913–1921
★ **BORN** Staunton, Va., Dec. 28, 1856
★ **INAUGURATED AS PRESIDENT** First term: Mar. 4, 1913 Second term: Mar. 5, 1917
★ **PARTY** Democratic
★ **DIED** Washington D.C., Feb. 3, 1924, age 67

WORLD WAR I

When war broke out in Europe in 1914, Wilson struggled to

Newspaper dated April 3, 1917

keep the United States out of the conflict. Germany refused to recognize the neutrality of U.S. ships until Wilson issued strong warnings. But in 1917, this agreement broke down, and it was discovered that Germany was trying to form an anti–American alliance with Mexico. Wilson was forced to ask Congress for a declaration of war. Over one million U.S. troops were sent to Europe. They were a decisive factor in the final collapse of Germany in November, 1918.

KEY EVENTS

1879 Woodrow Wilson graduates from Princeton University. **1885** Wilson and Ellen Axon marry. **1886** Wilson receives a Ph.D. from Johns Hopkins University, the only president to earn

this degree. **1902** Wilson is named president of Princeton University. **1910** Wilson is elected governor of New Jersey. **1912** Wilson defeats Theodore Roosevelt and William Taft in the

presidential election. **1913** The Seventeenth Amendment, establishing the direct election of U.S. senators by the voters of each state, is ratified; Congress passes the Underwood Act, which reduces tariffs; the Federal

A MAN OF PRINCIPLE

The son of a Presbyterian minister, Woodrow Wilson brought strong moral convictions to the presidency. Before entering political life, he was a popular professor and then president of Princeton University in New Jersey. As president, he found it hard to compromise his high moral principles. He is said to have admitted, "I feel sorry for those who disagree with me."

ELLEN WILSON

Gracious and intelligent, Ellen Wilson brought a quiet southern charm to the White House. She was an accomplished painter, a lover of literature, and a devoted mother to three daughters. When her husband embarked on his political career, she smoothed the way by helping him edit and rehearse speeches, as well as by advising him on the issues. Like many women in the 1910s, Mrs. Wilson believed in improving living conditions in the nation's cities. She supported a bill in Congress on slum clearance. Called the Ellen Wilson Bill, it passed in 1914, shortly before her death.

BIOGRAPHY

★ **YEARS AS FIRST LADY** 1913–1914
★ **BORN** Savannah, Ga., May 15, 1860
★ **MARRIED** Savannah, Ga., June 24, 1885
★ **CHILDREN** Margaret Woodrow, Jessie Woodrow, Eleanor Randolph
★ **DIED** Washington, D.C., Aug. 6, 1914, age 54

KEY EVENTS

Reserve Act is passed to regulate the nation's banking system.
1914 World War I begins in Europe and Wilson declares the United States' neutrality in the conflict; Ellen Wilson dies; the Clayton Antitrust Act bans monopolistic business practices and protects unions from antitrust prosecution.
1915 A German submarine sinks the ocean liner *Lusitania*, killing U.S. citizens onboard; Woodrow Wilson and Edith Bolling Galt marry.
1916 Congress passes the National Defense Act, increasing the size of the army and navy; Germany agrees to curtail submarine warfare; Wilson is reelected president.

WILSON VOTES FOR WOMEN

President Wilson was firmly behind the women's suffrage movement. Women had been campaigning for the right to vote since the mid–19th century. Wilson's support, along with women's involvement in the war effort, finally turned the tide of public opinion in their favor. In August, 1920, the Nineteenth Amendment granted all female U.S. citizens the right to vote.

Suffrage pin

EDITH WILSON

Edith Bolling received no formal schooling until her teenage years, but she would become one of America's most influential first ladies. Her first husband's sudden death in 1908 left her a wealthy widow. Years later, an encounter with the recently widowed Woodrow Wilson resulted in their marriage. When the president suffered a paralyzing stroke in 1919, Edith was accused of running the government single–handedly. She screened her ailing husband's visitors and mail. The press often thought her influence on the executive office was excessive and called it a "regency."

BIOGRAPHY

★ **YEARS AS FIRST LADY**
1915–1921
★ **BORN** Wytheville, Va.,
Oct. 15, 1872
★ **MARRIED** Washington, D.C.,
Dec. 18, 1915
★ **DIED** Washington, D.C.,
Dec. 28, 1961, age 89

KEY EVENTS

1917 Germany resumes submarine warfare, sinking U.S. ships; the United States enters World War I.
1918 More than one million American soldiers go to fight in Europe; Germany is defeated, and World War I ends.

1919 Wilson negotiates the Treaty of Versailles; Wilson suffers a stroke while touring the nation; the Eighteenth Amendment is passed, making the consumption of alcohol illegal.
1920 The U.S. Senate

rejects the Treaty of Versailles; the Nineteenth Amendment grants U.S. women the right to vote; Warren G. Harding is elected president.
1924 Woodrow Wilson dies.
1961 Edith Wilson dies.

HARDING

WARREN G. HARDING called for a return to a simpler, quieter way of life after World War I. Voters elected him by a wide margin. Harding yielded much of his executive power to Congress, which reduced taxes and placed quotas on immigration. Unfortunately, he delegated authority to advisors who proved to be dishonest, and scandals sullied his administration. Then, in 1923, Harding died suddenly.

BIOGRAPHY

★ **29TH PRESIDENT**
1921–1923
★ **BORN** Bloomington Grove, Ohio, Nov. 2, 1865
★ **PARTY** Republican
★ **DIED** San Francisco, Calif., Aug. 2, 1923, age 57

FLORENCE HARDING

Florence Kling was strong-willed and self-reliant. When her first husband abandoned her and their son, she supported herself by giving piano lessons. Years later, she met and married Warren Harding and took credit for managing his presidential campaign. Her reign as first lady was cut short by Warren's death.

BIOGRAPHY

★ **YEARS AS FIRST LADY**
1921–1923
★ **BORN** Marion, Ohio, Aug. 15, 1860
★ **MARRIED** Marion, Ohio, July 8, 1891
★ **CHILDREN** (from former marriage) Marshall deWolfe
★ **DIED** Marion, Ohio, Nov. 21, 1924, age 64

KEY EVENTS

1891 Warren Harding and Florence Kling marry.
1898 Harding is elected to Ohio state legislature.
1914 Harding is elected to U.S. Senate.
1920 Prohibition begins, making the sale and consumption of alcohol

illegal; Harding is elected president.
1921 Harding appoints Herbert Hoover secretary of commerce; Congress places quotas on immigration to the United States.
1922 Scandals emerge

involving members of Harding's administration; tariff rates rise to record heights.
1923 Harding dies while in office; Calvin Coolidge becomes president.
1924 Florence Harding dies.

COOLIDGE

CALVIN COOLIDGE became president upon the sudden death of Warren Harding. Coolidge was honest and thrifty and brought back a sense of trust to the presidency after the scandals of Harding's administration. The economy was undergoing a period of great prosperity, and the new president did not interfere with it, believing that less government was best. It did not matter to most Americans that Coolidge did little to change things. The president enjoyed afternoon naps and allegedly slept more hours a day than any other president.

BIOGRAPHY

★ **30TH PRESIDENT** 1923–1929
★ **BORN** Plymouth Notch, Vt., July 4, 1872
★ **PARTY** Republican
★ **DIED** Northampton, Mass., Jan. 5, 1933, age 60

STRAIGHT–LACED CAL

Calvin Coolidge was the son of a Vermont shopkeeper. He trained as a lawyer and held several political posts before becoming governor of Massachusetts. Coolidge was a reserved man and said he found meeting new people difficult. But his New England modesty and upright values served him well during his presidency.

KEY EVENTS

1895 Calvin Coolidge graduates from Amherst College.
1902 Grace Goodhue graduates from the University of Vermont.
1905 Coolidge and Goodhue marry.
1907 Coolidge enters the Massachusetts state legislature.
1913 President Wilson appoints Franklin Roosevelt assistant secretary of the navy.
1918 Coolidge is elected governor of Massachusetts.
1920 Coolidge is elected vice president.
1923 Coolidge becomes president after Warren Harding's sudden death.
1924 The National Origins Act is passed, establishing permanent immigration quotas; Coolidge is reelected president; Congress overrides Coolidge's veto

THE ROARING TWENTIES

Coolidge's "hands-off" approach to the economy encouraged speculation in the stock market and led to a boom time in the 1920s. With lots of money and work, a "live now, pay later" society emerged.

Women in particular discovered a new sense of freedom: they cut their hair, wore shorter skirts, and learned how to dance the Charleston.

Life magazine cover from the 1920s

GRACE COOLIDGE

Grace Coolidge attended the University of Vermont, and then taught at the Clarke School for the Deaf. After her marriage to Calvin, Grace stayed at home with their two sons. Warren Harding's death in 1923 catapulted Grace into the public eye. Despite the 1924 death of her younger son, Calvin, Jr., Grace managed to shine in the White House.

BIOGRAPHY

★ **YEARS AS FIRST LADY** 1923–1929
★ **BORN** Burlington, Vt., Jan. 3, 1879
★ **MARRIED** Burlington, Vt., Oct. 4, 1905
★ **CHILDREN** John, Calvin
★ **DIED** Northampton, Mass., July 8, 1957, age 78

Grace Coolidge with her pet raccoon named Rebecca

KEY EVENTS

and pays bonuses to WW I veterans.
1925 The Scopes trial, on teaching evolution in the classroom, takes place.
1926 Coolidge signs the Air Commerce Act, regulating the aviation industry.

1927 Coolidge vetoes a bill for the federal government to buy farm surpluses; Charles Lindbergh makes the first nonstop flight across the Atlantic Ocean.
1928 Coolidge declines to run for another term; fifteen nations, including the U.S.,

sign the Kellogg-Briand Pact, renouncing war as a way of resolving disputes; Herbert Hoover is elected president.
1933 Calvin Coolidge dies.
1957 Grace Coolidge dies.

HOOVER

HERBERT HOOVER seemed to be a perfect choice for president, being a self-made millionaire. However, only months after he took office, the stock market crashed, triggering the Great Depression. Businesses went bankrupt, and people lost their jobs. Many people unfairly blamed Hoover for the disaster. Hoover tried to rally the nation, but he did not think it was the government's responsibility to provide welfare relief. Although he eventually gave banks and businesses federal loans, he refused to help the destitute.

MOST LIKELY TO SUCCEED
Herbert Hoover was an American success story. Despite being orphaned as a child, Hoover became a wealthy mining engineer. During and after World War I, he served as an effective administrator of food and humanitarian aid in Europe and at home.

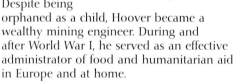

1932 campaign button

BIOGRAPHY

★ **31ST PRESIDENT** 1929–1933
★ **BORN** West Branch, Iowa, Aug. 10, 1874
★ **PARTY** Republican
★ **DIED** New York, N.Y., Oct. 20, 1964, age 90

KEY EVENTS

1895 Herbert Hoover graduates from Stanford University and goes to work as a mining engineer.

1898 Lou Henry graduates from Stanford University with a degree in geology.

1899 Hoover and Henry marry.

1917 President Wilson appoints Hoover head of the U.S. Food Administration to provide aid during World War I.

1921 President Harding appoints Hoover secretary

of commerce, a position he holds until 1928.

1922 Lou Hoover is elected national president of the Girl Scouts.

1928 Hoover is elected president.

1929 The stock market crashes and the Great

THE STOCK MARKET CRASH

On October 24, 1929, the New York Stock Exchange crashed, triggering the Great Depression. Fueled by unrestrained speculation, the great stock market crash caused a violent downward spiral in the American economy. Stock prices plummeted and many businesses were ruined. The day of the crash became known as "Black Thursday." Many people lost their jobs, as well as their life savings. President Hoover was blamed–unfairly, Lou thought–for the plight of the country and lost his bid for reelection.

LOU HOOVER

Equestrienne, hunter, taxidermist, and linguist–Lou was a woman of many interests. She was also the first woman to graduate with a geology degree from Stanford University. Shortly after completing her studies, she married Herbert Hoover, a mining engineer she had met at college. His business took them to posts around the world. During World War I and throughout the Great Depression, which began in 1929, Lou devoted herself to public service. While in the White House, she supported the struggles of women and minorities in gaining equal rights.

BIOGRAPHY

★ **YEARS AS FIRST LADY** 1929–1933
★ **BORN** Waterloo, Iowa, Mar. 29, 1874
★ **MARRIED** Monterey, Calif., Feb. 10, 1899
★ **CHILDREN** Herbert Clark, Allan Henry
★ **DIED** New York, N.Y., Jan. 7, 1944, age 69

KEY EVENTS

Depression begins.
1930 Hoover signs the Hawley-Smoot Tariff, which raises taxes on imported goods and angers international trading partners.
1931 Lou Hoover addresses the nations' Girl Scouts by radio, becoming the first presidential wife to use radio to promote her views.
1932 Hoover establishes the Reconstruction Finance Corporation to provide loans to failing businesses; unemployed WW I veterans march on Washington, D.C., and federal troops are sent in to disperse them; Franklin D. Roosevelt defeats Hoover in the presidential election.
1944 Lou Hoover dies.
1964 Herbert Hoover dies.

ROOSEVELT

FRANKLIN D. ROOSEVELT became president in the midst of the Great Depression. To bring the country out of its economic woes, he implemented revolutionary programs of aid – called the New Deal – for businessmen, farmers, workers, and the unemployed alike. Roosevelt's personal history meant he could empathize with the disadvantaged. A bout of polio in middle age left him unable to walk unaided for the rest of his life. Roosevelt also led the nation through World War II.

BIOGRAPHY

★ **32ND PRESIDENT** 1933–1945
★ **BORN** Hyde Park, N.Y., Jan. 30, 1882
★ **INAUGURATED AS PRESIDENT**
  First term: Mar. 4, 1933
  Second term: Jan. 20, 1937
  Third term: Jan. 20, 1941
  Fourth term: Jan. 20, 1945
★ **PARTY** Democratic
★ **DIED** Warm Springs, Ga.,
  Apr. 12, 1945, age 63

ROOSEVELT SPEAKS TO THE NATION

In 1933, the nation's banking system collapsed. In a memorable speech, Roosevelt promised to deal with the crisis, announcing: "The only thing we have to fear is fear itself." In the first of many "fireside chat" radio broadcasts, Roosevelt urged people to trust the nation's banks, and an anxious nation responded.

KEY EVENTS

1903 Franklin D. Roosevelt graduates from Harvard University.
1905 Franklin Roosevelt and Anna Eleanor Roosevelt marry.
1910 Roosevelt is elected to the New York state legislature.

1913 President Wilson appoints Roosevelt the secretary of the navy.
1921 Roosevelt is stricken with polio.
1928 Roosevelt is elected governor of New York.
1932 Roosevelt is elected president.

1933 The Midwest and Great Plains are struck with drought and dust storms that drive thousands from itheir farms; after taking office, Roosevelt declares a "banking holiday" to shore up the nation's banking system.

ELEANOR ROOSEVELT

Raised by her grandmother and educated at the best private schools, Eleanor married her charming fifth cousin Franklin Delano Roosevelt. After bearing six children, one of whom died in infancy, she devoted her life to politics, advancing Franklin's career after he contracted polio. During the Great Depression, Mrs. Roosevelt's trips across the United States, as well as her weekly radio broadcasts, brought hope to millions of suffering Americans.

BIOGRAPHY

★ **YEARS AS FIRST LADY**
  1933–1945
★ **BORN** New York, N.Y.,
  Oct. 11, 1884
★ **MARRIED** New York, N.Y.,
  Mar. 17, 1905
★ **CHILDREN** Anna Eleanor,
  James, Franklin Delano, Jr.
  (died in infancy), Elliott,
  Franklin Delano, Jr.,
  John Aspinwall
★ **DIED** New York, N.Y.,
  Nov. 7, 1962, age 78

*Postage stamp honoring
Eleanor Roosevelt*

THE FIRST LADY AS SOCIAL ACTIVIST

Called the First Lady of the World by President Harry S. Truman, Eleanor Roosevelt is considered one of the greatest humanitarians of the twentieth century. As first lady, she worked tirelessly to improve the lives of those in need. After being widowed at age sixty, she continued to serve her country as the U.S. delegate to the United Nations. Eleanor was also a firm advocate of civil rights and fought to end segregation and discrimination. Remembered for her great compassion, Mrs. Roosevelt remains one of the most respected first ladies.

KEY EVENTS

1933 Roosevelt makes his first "fireside chat" radio broadcast; Roosevelt appoints Frances Perkins secretary of labor; she is the first woman appointed to the president's cabinet; New Deal legislation provides new federal relief programs; the Twenty-First Amendment passes and ends Prohibition. **1935** The Social Security Act is passed, creating a national pension system; the Wagner Act is passed, protecting labor's right to unionize.

1936 Eleanor Roosevelt begins her newspaper column, "My Day"; Franklin Roosevelt is reelected president.
1939 Germany invades Poland; World War II breaks out in Europe; the United States remains neutral.

Eleanor Roosevelt serves food at a soup kitchen in 1932

A NEW DEAL FOR ALL

Roosevelt called his program of aid and reform the New Deal, and one of his first goals was to put people back to work. He was concerned with helping what he called the forgotten man; that is, the ordinary worker who was unemployed and starving. He set about establishing federal programs for work projects and financial aid–solutions President Hoover had refused to contemplate.

FIGHTING A WORLD WAR

In 1940, Roosevelt won a historic third term. No president before had ever been in office longer than eight years. Roosevelt's leadership was still needed to pull America out of the Depression. Then on the heels of one crisis came another–World War II. Ironically, the war effort put an end to the country's economic problems. The United States entered the war in December, 1941, after Japan attacked the U.S. naval base at Pearl Harbor. During the next four years, Roosevelt set up programs for raising and training the millions of men and women needed for the armed forces.

WWII poster

KEY EVENTS

1940 The federal government institutes the first peacetime military draft in U.S. history; Roosevelt is reelected president.
1941 Congress passes the Lend-Lease bill to supply arms to Great Britain; Germany invades the Soviet Union; on Dec. 7, Japan attacks U.S. military bases at Pearl Harbor in Hawaii, and the United States enters WW II.
1942 The "Manhattan Project," the top-secret U.S. research project to develop the atomic bomb, begins.
1943 Soviets defeat the Germans at the Battle of Stalingrad.
1944 The D-Day invasion, an Allied operation led by General

THE HOME FRONT

Once America had entered World War II, millions of men and women were needed to serve in the armed forces. On the home front, this left many jobs to be filled. The government launched poster campaigns urging U.S. citizens to work for the war effort. Roosevelt put his energy into getting the nation's factories to retool for war production.

This poster quotes F.D.R.

THE BIG THREE

In November, 1943, Roosevelt met with the Allied leaders, Winston Churchill, the prime minister of Great Britain, and the Soviet Union's premier, Joseph Stalin. The Big Three discussed their strategy for the planned joint invasion of German-occupied France. Stalin was anxious for this to happen soon to take the pressure off the Russian front. The D-Day invasion did not take place until June 6, 1944. Organized by General Dwight D. Eisenhower, it was a success and led to the liberation of France and the final defeat of Germany. In the same year, Roosevelt won reelection. The war, though, had taken its toll on Roosevelt's health. He died in April, 1945, a month before the German surrender.

KEY EVENTS

Dwight D. Eisenhower, liberates German-occupied France and leads to the final defeat of Germany the following year; Roosevelt is reelected president.

1945 Franklin Roosevelt dies and his vice

president, Harry S. Truman, enters the White House; Germany surrenders; atomic bombs are dropped on the Japanese cities of Hiroshima and Nagasaki; Japan surrenders and World War II ends.

1946 President Truman

appoints Eleanor Roosevelt a delegate to the United Nations.

1961 President Kennedy appoints Eleanor Roosevelt head of the Commission on the Status of Women.

1962 Eleanor Roosevelt dies.

TRUMAN

HARRY S. TRUMAN had global decisions to make upon assuming the presidency after Roosevelt's sudden death in 1945. The war in Europe was drawing to a close, but the Japanese refused to surrender. Ultimately, Truman ordered two atomic bombs to be dropped on Japan. Within days, the war was over. Peacetime brought new challenges. Truman now faced such problems as how to stop the spread of communism that led to war in Korea.

THE TRUMAN DOCTRINE

At the end of World War II, Joseph Stalin established communist governments in Eastern European countries to protect the Soviet Union. Truman became concerned about the spread of communism. In 1947, he announced his Truman Doctrine, which promised U.S. support to all nations fighting communism. The Cold War between the United States and the Soviet Union had begun.

BIOGRAPHY

★ **33RD PRESIDENT** 1945–1953
★ **BORN** Lamar, Mo., May 8, 1884
★ **INAUGURATED AS PRESIDENT**
First term: Apr. 12, 1945
Second term: Jan. 20, 1949
★ **PARTY** Democratic
★ **DIED** Kansas City, Mo.,
Dec. 26, 1972, age 88

1949 inauguration badge

KEY EVENTS

1919 Harry S. Truman and Elizabeth (Bess) Wallace marry.
1939 World War II begins in Europe.
1941 The United States enters WW II.
1944 Truman is elected vice president.

1945 Franklin Roosevelt dies; Truman becomes president; Germany surrenders and the war in Europe is over; U.S. scientists detonate the world's first atomic bomb; less than a month later Truman decides to drop atomic bombs on

Japan; Japan surrenders and World War II is over.
1947 The Truman Doctrine is announced; Taft-Hartley Act is passed, restricting union activities; the Marshall Plan, providing U.S. financial aid to rebuild non-communist western

THE KOREAN WAR

When communist North Korea attempted to seize control of South Korea in June, 1950, fears of the spread of communism led Truman to send U.S. troops into a country on the other side of the world. When U.S. forces, under the command of General Douglas MacArthur, crossed the border and invaded North Korea, the communist Chinese government sent vast numbers of troops into action. This war lasted until 1953.

BESS TRUMAN

After Harry Truman left the White House, he declared that his wife had been his "chief advisor" and a full partner. Indeed, Bess had worked alongside her husband even before he entered politics, and when he became a U.S. senator in 1935, she willingly left her hometown of Independence, Missouri, to take up life in the nation's capital. There, she became a paid staff member in Harry's office. When Truman took up the challenge of running the country, his wife faced the predicament of unwanted fame. Bess, who disliked social functions and held no press conferences, was respected as a no-nonsense woman and loyal wife. Harry's nickname for her was "The Boss."

BIOGRAPHY

★ YEARS AS FIRST LADY 1945–1953
★ BORN Independence, Mo., Feb. 13, 1885
★ MARRIED Independence, Mo., June 28, 1919
★ CHILDREN Margaret
★ DIED Independence, Mo., Oct. 18, 1982, age 97

KEY EVENTS

European nations, is established.

1948 The Soviet Union blockades Berlin, Germany, hoping to drive Allied troops out of the city; Truman is elected president.

1949 The Soviet blockade of Berlin ends; West and East Germany are established; the Soviet Union explodes an atomic bomb.

1950 The Korean War begins.

1951 Ethel and Julius Rosenberg are accused of being part of a Soviet spy ring; they are convicted of treason and executed in 1953.

1952 Dwight D. Eisenhower is elected president.

1953 The Korean War ends.

1972 Harry Truman dies.

1982 Bess Truman dies.

EISENHOWER

DWIGHT D. EISENHOWER was a World War II military leader, and his eight years in the White House were years of peace and prosperity for most Americans. Eisenhower brought an end to the Korean War in 1953. He also attempted to improve relations with the Soviet Union with a series of cultural exchanges. These ended, though, when a U.S. spy plane was shot down in Soviet air space. In domestic affairs, Eisenhower was forced to use federal troops to end the segregation of white and black Americans.

BIOGRAPHY

★ **34TH PRESIDENT** 1953–1961
★ **BORN** Denison, Tex., Oct. 14, 1890
★ **INAUGURATED AS PRESIDENT** First term: Jan. 20, 1953 Second term: Jan. 21, 1957
★ **PARTY** Republican
★ **DIED** Washington, D.C., Mar. 28, 1969, age 78

LIKABLE IKE

"I Like Ike" became one of the most memorable campaign slogans of all time. Eisenhower's ready smile and relaxed personality ensured his landslide victory in the presidential election of 1952.

"I Like Ike" buttons were worn everywhere—even by those who usually voted Democratic.

KEY EVENTS

1915 Dwight D. Eisenhower graduates from West Point.
1916 Dwight Eisenhower and Marie (Mamie) Geneva Doud marry.
1943 During WW II, Eisenhower is named commander of allied forces in Europe.
1945 President Truman names Eisenhower army chief of staff.
1950 Senator Joseph McCarthy begins to level charges of communist infiltration in the federal government and gains major media coverage.
1952 Eisenhower retires from the army after 37 years to run for president; Eisenhower is elected with Richard Nixon as vice president.
1953 Eisenhower ends

LITTLE ROCK

During Eisenhower's presidency, civil rights became a pressing issue. After the Supreme Court ruled in 1954 that segregating black and white citizens was illegal, cities began desegregating their schools. But in the South there was strong resistance. In 1957, Governor Orval Faubus of Little Rock, Arkansas, called out the state's National Guard to prevent a group of black students from enrolling in an all-white high school. Eisenhower was forced to act. He sent federal troops to make sure that the students were escorted safely to school.

MAMIE EISENHOWER

As the wife of a career military officer, Mamie Eisenhower had years of experience in handling challenging social situations. This served her well when her husband became president. Mamie, a devoted wife, mother, and hostess, appealed to Americans, and particularly to housewives who felt they had something in common with her. On the campaign trail, she became a celebrity in her own right. As first lady, Mamie tackled her role with enthusiasm, ran the White House with military precision, and charmed the nation at the same time.

BIOGRAPHY

★ **YEARS AS FIRST LADY** 1953–1961
★ **BORN** Boone, Iowa, Nov. 14, 1896
★ **MARRIED** Denver, Colo., July 1, 1916
★ **CHILDREN** Doud Dwight, John Sheldon
★ **DIED** Gettysburg, Penn., Nov. 11, 1979, age 82

KEY EVENTS

the Korean War.
1954 The Supreme Court rules racial segregation in public schools is unconstitutional; McCarthy is censured by the Senate, ending his communist witch-hunts.
1955 Rosa Parks refuses to give up her seat on a bus, sparking a major civil rights boycott that brings the civil rights movement national attention.
1957 The Soviet Union launches the first satellite into space; Eisenhower sends in federal troops to safely desegregate an all-white high school in Little Rock, Arkansas.
1960 John F. Kennedy is elected president.
1969 Dwight Eisenhower dies.
1979 Mamie Eisenhower dies.

KENNEDY

JOHN F. KENNEDY, at the age of 43, was the youngest president ever elected. Handsome and witty, Kennedy and his young family brought youth, vigor, and vitality to the White House. As part of his New Frontier program, he proposed civil rights legislation and urban renewal. He founded the Peace Corps, a way for young people to promote goodwill in developing countries. Kennedy resolved a tense stand-off with the Soviet Union over nuclear testing. His term of office, though, was tragically brief. In 1963, Kennedy was assassinated.

ELECTIONEERING

During his political career, Kennedy never lost an election. He enjoyed politicking, and in 1960, he ran for president with great enthusiasm. Touting the slogan, "Let's get this country moving again," Kennedy flew around the United States wooing the voters with his confidence and charm.

Inaugural pin

BIOGRAPHY

★ **35TH PRESIDENT** 1961–1963
★ **BORN** Brookline, Mass., May 29, 1917
★ **INAUGURATED AS PRESIDENT** Jan. 20, 1961
★ **PARTY** Democratic
★ **DIED** Dallas, Tex., Nov. 22, 1963, age 46

KEY EVENTS

1940 John F. Kennedy graduates from Harvard University.
1941 Kennedy joins the Navy and serves in WW II.
1946 Kennedy is elected to U.S. House of Representatives.

1951 Jacqueline Bouvier graduates from George Washington University.
1952 Bouvier takes a job with the *Washington Times-Herald*; Kennedy is elected to U.S. Senate.
1953 Kennedy and Bouvier marry.

1960 Kennedy is elected president, with Lyndon B. Johnson as vice president.
1961 A U.S.-directed invasion of Cuba fails; Kennedy establishes the Peace Corps to aid in international development.
1962 Jackie Kennedy

AMERICA MOURNS

On November 22, 1963, President Kennedy was shot and killed while riding in a motorcade through Dallas, Texas. Jackie personally directed the funeral, broadcast on television, and displayed remarkable dignity and composure to a stunned country that shared her grief.

Police arrested 24-year-old Lee Harvey Oswald for the murder, but he was shot two days later by Jack Ruby while in police custody. Though it was established that Oswald had acted alone, conspiracy theories have surrounded Kennedy's assassination ever since.

JACQUELINE KENNEDY

The glamorous and privileged Jacqueline Kennedy–Jackie to the American public–became a symbol of style and elegance during the 1960s. Young, intelligent, and beautiful, she may have been her husband's greatest asset during his presidential campaign. She met her future husband while working as a news photographer. Jackie used her knowledge of art to initiate a restoration project that turned the White House into a national showcase and welcomed noted writers, scientists, and politicians to participate in state receptions.

BIOGRAPHY

★ YEARS AS FIRST LADY 1961–1963
★ BORN Southampton, N.Y., July 28, 1929
★ MARRIED Newport, R.I., Sept. 12, 1953
★ CHILDREN Caroline Bouvier, John Fitzgerald, Patrick Bouvier (died in infancy)
★ DIED New York, N.Y., May 19, 1994, age 64

KEY EVENTS

leads a nationally televised tour of the White House; President Kennedy orders a blockade of Cuba; after a tense standoff, the Soviet Union backs down.
1963 Martin Luther King, Jr., delivers his famous "I have a dream" speech at a

civil rights march in Washington, D.C.; the United States, the Soviet Union, and Great Britain sign a treaty limiting the testing of nuclear weapons; Kennedy is assassinated in Dallas, Texas; Lyndon Johnson becomes president;

Kennedy assassin Lee Harvey Oswald is shot and killed by Jack Ruby.
1968 Jackie Kennedy marries Aristotle Onassis.
1975 Aristotle Onassis dies.
1994 Jacqueline Kennedy Onassis dies.

JOHNSON

LYNDON B. JOHNSON became president after the death of John F. Kennedy. This Texan had grand designs for his country. He declared a "war on poverty" and introduced extensive social legislation. Although he sought to promote racial harmony, race riots flared up in many cities. His presidency also saw escalating protests against U.S. involvement in the Vietnam War. Johnson became so discouraged that he refused to seek reelection.

JOHNSON'S DREAM

Johnson wanted to end racial hatred and poverty, and he succeeded in getting his program of social legislation through Congress. The Civil Rights Act of 1964 banned racial segregation in public places. The Voting Rights Act of 1965 outlawed voting requirements that had robbed many African-Americans of the right to vote.

Sheet music for "The Great Society March"

BIOGRAPHY

★ **36TH PRESIDENT** 1963–1969
★ **BORN** Near Stonewall, Tex., Aug. 27, 1908
★ **INAUGURATED AS PRESIDENT**
  First term: Nov. 22, 1963
  Second term: Jan. 20, 1965
★ **PARTY** Democratic
★ **DIED** San Antonio, Tex., Jan. 22, 1973, age 64

KEY EVENTS

1930 Lyndon B. Johnson graduates from Southwest Texas Teachers College.
1933 Claudia (Lady Bird) Taylor graduates from the University of Texas at Austin.
1934 Johnson and Taylor marry.

1937 Johnson is elected to U.S. House of Representatives.
1941–42 Johnson serves in U.S. Navy during World War II.
1948 Johnson is elected to U.S. Senate.
1960 Johnson is elected

vice president.
1963 Johnson becomes president after Kennedy's assassination.
1964 Tax cut is passed; the Civil Rights Act is passed; Johnson is reelected president.
1965 Civil rights march

THE VIETNAM WAR

When Johnson became president, about 16,000 U.S. soldiers were in South Vietnam helping to stop the communists in the North from taking over the entire country. He was forced to order bombing raids and then sent in combat troops.

With American casualties mounting, Johnson despaired of finding a quick and honorable end to the war. Antiwar protests soon became a mass movement, as America's youth grew disenchanted with Johnson's war policies.

LADY BIRD JOHNSON

Nicknamed Lady Bird, Claudia Taylor graduated in the top 10 percent of her college class at the age of twenty. Lady Bird's gracious manner provided the perfect balance to Lyndon Johnson's often harsh and unpredictable behavior. After supporting him through many congressional elections, she campaigned exhaustively for the 1960 Kennedy–Johnson presidential ticket. As first lady, Mrs. Johnson created an awareness of the environment and promoted programs to improve conditions in poverty–stricken neighborhoods.

BIOGRAPHY

★ **YEARS AS FIRST LADY** 1963–1969
★ **BORN** Karnack, Tex., Dec. 12, 1912
★ **MARRIED** San Antonio, Tex., Nov. 17, 1934
★ **CHILDREN** Lynda Bird, Luci Baines

KEY EVENTS

from Selma to Montgomery, Alabama, takes place; the Voting Rights Act is passed; Medicaid and Medicare, health insurance for the elderly and poor, is established; Head Start, preschool for the poor, is established; Johnson authorizes massive bombing raids in Vietnam; the first combat troops arrive in South Vietnam; antiwar protests begin; Congress passes the Highway Beautification Bill, with the support of Lady Bird. **1968** More than 500,000 U.S. troops are fighting in Vietnam; Johnson announces he will not run for reelection; Martin Luther King, Jr., is assassinated; race riots erupt in Washington, D.C. **1973** Lyndon Johnson dies.

NIXON

RICHARD M. NIXON experienced the highs and lows of politics like few people ever have. He served as vice president to Eisenhower, but lost a close 1960 presidential election to Kennedy. Just when his political career seemed to be over, Nixon was elected president in 1968. He showed a flair for foreign diplomacy and brought an end to U.S. military involvement in Vietnam. Despite all of its successes, Nixon's administration is remembered primarily for the Watergate scandal. Faced with impeachment, Richard Nixon became the first U.S. president to resign.

BIOGRAPHY

- ★ **37TH PRESIDENT** 1969–1974
- ★ **BORN** Yorba Linda, Calif., Jan. 9, 1913
- ★ **INAUGURATED AS PRESIDENT**
  First term: Jan. 20, 1969
  Second term: Jan. 20, 1973
- ★ **PARTY** Republican
- ★ **DIED** New York, N.Y., Apr. 22, 1994, age 81

COLD WAR POLITICS

When Nixon sensed a rift between between America's cold war enemies, China and the Soviet Union, he decided to open negotiations with Chairman Mao, the Chinese leader. Cultural and political exchanges between China and the United States followed in 1971. The next year, Nixon continued this policy of détente, or relaxation, by visiting the Soviet Union. At the end of this trip, he announced plans for a joint U.S.–Soviet program to limit nuclear arms.

KEY EVENTS

1940 Richard M. Nixon and Thelma (Pat) Catherine Ryan marry.
1946 Nixon is elected to U.S. House of Representatives.
1950 Nixon is elected to U.S. Senate.
1952 Nixon is elected

vice president and serves two terms with President Dwight D. Eisenhower.
1960 Nixon is defeated by John F. Kennedy in a close presidential election.
1968 Nixon is elected president with Spiro Agnew as vice president.

1969 Astronauts Neil Armstrong and Edwin "Buzz" Aldrin are the first people to walk on the moon.
1970 The National Guard fires on an antiwar demonstration at Kent State University and four

THE WATERGATE SCANDAL

In June, 1972, five burglars were caught planting bugging devices in the Democratic party headquarters at the Watergate complex in Washington, D.C. Nixon denied any role in these illegal activities as they were being investigated. Witnesses testified that Nixon directed a cover-up. The release of taped conversations in the Oval Office incriminated Nixon, and three articles of impeachment were issued against him. On August 9, 1973, Nixon resigned the presidency.

IMPEACH NIXON!

Pin from Watergate era

PAT NIXON

Pat Nixon lost both her parents by the age of eighteen and valiantly worked her way through college during the Great Depression. Although she disliked politics, she dutifully campaigned for her husband, appealing to women voters by representing the ideals of home and family. When Richard Nixon won his bid for the presidency in 1968, Pat became a goodwill ambassador, traveling around the world on diplomatic missions. She continued the White House renovation started by Jacqueline Kennedy, adding more than five hundred antiques and pieces of art.

Pat and Richard Nixon at daughter Tricia's White House wedding

BIOGRAPHY

★ YEARS AS FIRST LADY 1969–1974
★ BORN Ely, Nev., Mar. 16, 1912
★ MARRIED Riverside, Calif., June 21, 1940
★ CHILDREN Patricia, Julie
★ DIED Park Ridge, N.J., June 22, 1993, age 81

KEY EVENTS

protesters are killed.
1971 Nixon makes an official state visit to China.
1972 Nixon negotiates a U.S.-Soviet program to limit nuclear arms; Watergate break-in occurs; Nixon is reelected president.
1973 Senate investigates the Watergate affair; Nixon negotiates a ceasefire in the Vietnam War; U.S. combat troops are withdrawn from Vietnam; Spiro Agnew resigns as vice president amid charges of bribery and extortion; Nixon appoints Gerald Ford vice president.
1974 Articles of impeachment are issued against Nixon; Nixon resigns; Ford becomes president; Ford pardons Nixon.
1993 Pat Nixon dies.
1994 Richard Nixon dies.

FORD

GERALD R. FORD was appointed vice president by Richard Nixon in 1973 and then sworn in as president in 1974 when Nixon resigned. Ford announced: "Our long national nightmare is over" and immediately set about restoring credibility to America's highest office. In a controversial gesture to heal the nation (and also to prevent a lengthy trial), he pardoned Nixon of any wrongdoing. He also offered amnesty to Vietnam War deserters and draft-dodgers. A highlight of Ford's presidency was the 1976 Bicentennial celebration of the nation's founding.

THE FOOTBALL STAR

Ford enjoyed a dazzling football career at the University of Michigan. Afterward, in 1941, he graduated in law from Yale University. Ford's nickname was "Mr. Nice Guy," but he also had a reputation for being a patient thinker. Lyndon B. Johnson unkindly remarked that Ford had played too much football without his helmet on.

BIOGRAPHY

★ **38TH PRESIDENT**
1974–1977
★ **BORN** Omaha, Nebr.,
July 14, 1913
★ **INAUGURATED AS
PRESIDENT** Aug. 9, 1974
★ **PARTY** Republican

KEY EVENTS

1935 Gerald Ford, a college football player, graduates from the University of Michigan.
1941 Ford graduates from Yale University Law School.
1948 Ford and Elizabeth (Betty)

Bloomer marry; Ford is elected to U.S. House of Representatives.
1973 President Nixon appoints Ford vice president.
1974 Nixon resigns and Ford becomes president; Ford appoints Nelson

Rockefeller vice president; Ford offers amnesty for Vietnam War draft dodgers and deserters; Ford pardons former president Nixon; Betty Ford declares her support for abortion rights and the ERA; Betty Ford

EVACUATION OF SAIGON

The peace treaty negotiated by President Nixon in Vietnam did not last long. In April, 1975, communist forces captured the city of Saigon in South Vietnam.

Prior to the invasion, hundreds of American citizens and Vietnamese refugees were airlifted to safety, ending U.S. involvement in Vietnam.

BETTY FORD

A direct and likable first lady, Betty Ford was not afraid to speak honestly about issues that affected her personal life. Entering the White House suddenly after Nixon's resignation, Betty declared her support of the arts, the elderly, and, most shockingly, the Equal Rights Amendment (ERA)—feminist legislation that her husband strongly opposed. Her frank discussions about her battle with breast cancer, a subject that previously had been avoided in public, inspired many women to talk about their own experiences. After leaving the White House, Betty admitted to having a dependence on painkillers and alcohol. She sought professional help and founded the now-famous Betty Ford Center for Drug and Alcohol Rehabilitation in Rancho Mirage, California.

BIOGRAPHY

★ YEARS AS FIRST LADY
1974–1977
★ BORN Chicago, Ill.,
Apr. 8, 1918
★ MARRIED Grand Rapids,
Mich., Oct. 15, 1948
★ CHILDREN Michael
Gerald, John Gardner,
Steven Meigs,
Susan Elizabeth

KEY EVENTS

undergoes breast cancer surgery and goes public with her illness.
1975 With the evacuation of Saigon, U.S. involvement in Vietnam ends; Helsinki summit improves U.S.-Soviet relations; Secretary of

State Henry Kissinger negotiates a ceasefire between Israel and Egypt; Betty Ford is named *Time* magazine's "Woman of the Year."
1976 The United States celebrates the Bicentennial of the nation's founding;

Ford appoints George Bush director of the Central Intelligence Agency (CIA); Ford loses the presidential election to Jimmy Carter.
1980 Ford declines to serve as Ronald Reagan's vice president.

CARTER

JIMMY CARTER was voted into office in 1976 by an American public that wanted change. Burdened by the high cost of living and tired of scandal–ridden politics, they saw Carter as a fresh new face in town. Carter touted his human decency, while promising to fix the economy. As a diplomat, he achieved peace in the Middle East. Yet stemming high inflation proved to be a difficult task. Nor could he do much to ease the energy crisis. Carter meant well, but Americans soon came to regard him as ineffective. Since leaving office, Carter has become a respected public figure through his work for international peace.

CARTER DELIVERS CAMP DAVID ACCORD

In 1978, Carter played the role of international peacemaker, hosting talks between President Sadat of Egypt and Prime Minister Begin of Israel. After nearly two weeks at Camp David, Maryland, peace accords were signed, ending the state of war between the two countries that had existed since 1948. Carter was widely praised for his skill and determination; he had achieved a stunning breakthrough.

BIOGRAPHY

★ **39TH PRESIDENT** 1977–1981
★ **BORN** Plains, Ga., Oct. 1, 1924
★ **INAUGURATED AS PRESIDENT** Jan. 20, 1977
★ **PARTY** Democratic

KEY EVENTS

1946 Jimmy Carter graduates from the U.S. Naval Academy; Carter and Rosalynn Smith marry.

1953 After his father's death, Carter resigns from the navy and returns home to run his family's peanut business with Rosalynn.

1962 Carter is elected to Georgia state legislature.

1970 Carter is elected governor of Georgia.

1976 The United States celebrates its Bicentennial; Carter is elected president.

1977 The Department of Energy is created; U.S.-Panama treaty is signed, returning the Panama Canal to Panama in 1999; Rosalynn Carter serves as honorary chair of President's Commission on Mental Health.

THE HOSTAGE CRISIS

In November, 1979, militant Iranians took over the U.S. embassy in Tehran and held sixty-six Americans hostage. The captors opposed U.S. policy, which refused to officially recognize Iranian leader Ayatollah Khomeini. Carter's efforts to free the hostages failed and weakened his presidency. The Americans were finally released on his last day in office.

Banner honoring the freed hostages

ROSALYNN CARTER

Rosalynn Smith was not yet nineteen when she married U.S. Navy midshipman Jimmy Carter. When Jimmy returned to Georgia to take over his father's peanut business, Rosalynn worked alongside him. Later, when he was elected governor of Georgia, she confidently entered the world of politics. Rosalynn was her husband's most trusted advisor during their White House years. As first lady, she attended cabinet meetings and discussed issues and policies with foreign leaders and was, therefore, criticized for exceeding the limits of her position.

BIOGRAPHY

★ YEARS AS FIRST LADY 1977–1981
★ BORN Plains, Ga., Aug. 18, 1927
★ MARRIED Plains, Ga., July 7, 1946
★ CHILDREN John William, James Earl III, Jeffrey, Amy Lynn

KEY EVENTS

1978 Egypt-Israel peace accord is signed; in a revolution, the Shah of Iran is removed from leadership.
1979 Militant Iranians take U.S. embassy staff in Tehran hostage; Soviet Union invades Afghanistan.
1980 A failed rescue of the U.S. hostages in Iran leaves eight servicemen dead; U.S. boycotts summer Olympics in Moscow, protesting invasion of Afghanistan; Iran-Iraq War begins; U.S. inflation remains high; Carter is defeated by Ronald Reagan in the presidential election.
1981 The hostages in Iran are released on Carter's last day in office.
1994 Carter negotiates with North Korea to stop nuclear weapons development and helps negotiate peace in Haiti.

REAGAN

At age 69, **RONALD REAGAN** was the oldest president to enter the White House. A former movie actor, he became known as the "Great Communicator" because of his ease in front of the television camera. Reagan believed that by supporting business, prosperity would filter down to all levels of society. Although inflation was reduced, by the end of the 1980s the national debt had doubled. Despite a major political scandal and problems in the U.S. space program, Reagan remained an extremely popular president.

Campaign belt buckle

BIOGRAPHY

★ **40TH PRESIDENT** 1981–1989
★ **BORN** Tampico, Ill., Feb. 6, 1911
★ **INAUGURATED AS PRESIDENT**
   First term: Jan. 20, 1981
   Second term: Jan. 20, 1985
★ **PARTY** Republican
★ **CHILDREN** (from first marriage to Jane Wyman) Maureen, Michael Edward (from second marriage to Nancy Reagan) Patti Davis, Ronald Prescott

SHUTTLE DISASTER

America's space program was set back when the Challenger space shuttle exploded shortly after liftoff on January 28, 1986. All seven members of the flight were killed, including schoolteacher Christa McAuliffe, who planned to broadcast lessons from space.

KEY EVENTS

1932 Ronald Reagan graduates from Eureka College.
1937 Reagan begins his acting career at Warner Brothers studio.
1940 Reagan marries actress Jane Wyman.
1943 Nancy Davis graduates from Smith College.
1948 Reagan and Wyman divorce.
1952 Reagan and Nancy Davis marry.
1966 Reagan is elected governor of California.
1980 Reagan is elected president with George Bush as vice president.
1981 Reagan is shot and seriously wounded in an assassination attempt; Reagan appoints Sandra Day O'Connor as the first female Supreme Court justice.

THE IRAN CONTRA AFFAIR

In November, 1986, a scandal emerged that cast a shadow over Reagan's second term. In an attempt to secure the release of captive American citizens, the National Security Council had secretly and illegally sold weapons to Iran. To make matters worse, the money from the arms deals had been used to aid the anticommunist contras in Nicaragua–despite such aid being outlawed by Congress. While Reagan declared that he knew nothing about these deals, his credibility suffered.

NANCY REAGAN

Nancy Reagan was fiercely protective of her husband and often faulted for having too much power over affairs of state. After marrying Reagan in 1952, she retired from her acting career to raise their two children. As first lady, Nancy was criticized for redecorating the family living quarters and spending large sums on official receptions. Mrs. Reagan countered such attacks with humor and quickly changed her image to reflect her social concerns. She adopted drug abuse as her cause, encouraging children to "Just Say No" to drugs.

BIOGRAPHY

★ **YEARS AS FIRST LADY** 1981–1989
★ **BORN** New York, N.Y., July 6, 1921
★ **MARRIED** San Fernando Valley, Calif., March 4, 1952

KEY EVENTS

1982 U.S. troops are sent to Lebanon to help keep the peace.
1983 The United States invades Grenada.
1984 U.S. troops are withdrawn from Lebanon; Reagan is reelected president.

1985 Congress passes legislation to reduce the federal budget deficit.
1986 The Challenger space shuttle explodes, killing all onboard; Iran-Contra scandal erupts.
1987 The United States and Soviet Union sign a

treaty reducing the number of nuclear weapons in Europe.
1988 George Bush is elected president.
1993 Reagan announces he has Alzheimer's disease and retreats from public life.

BUSH

GEORGE BUSH had to grapple with foreign affairs throughout his presidency. In 1989, he ordered troops into Panama to oust the corrupt dictator, General Manuel Noriega. A year later, he was rallying a multinational coalition to force Iraq out of neighboring Kuwait. When the American-led forces won the Persian Gulf War, Bush emerged a popular hero. The collapse of the Soviet Union, ending the Cold War, only strengthened Bush's image as the world's most powerful leader. Yet as the country went into economic recession, Bush's popularity eroded.

BIOGRAPHY

★ 41ST PRESIDENT 1989–1993
★ BORN Milton, Mass.,
   June 12, 1924
★ INAUGURATED AS PRESIDENT
   Jan. 20, 1989
★ PARTY Republican

EAST REJOINS WEST AT LAST

On November, 9, 1989, East Germans began to tear down the Berlin Wall that had divided East from West Berlin for 28 years. This symbolic event heralded the end of the Cold War. By 1990, Germany was reunified and the communist governments in Eastern Europe had begun to collapse.

KEY EVENTS

1942 George Bush enters the U.S. Navy and serves in World War II.
1945 Bush and Barbara Pierce marry.
1948 Bush graduates from Yale University.
1953 Robin Bush, daughter of George and Barbara, dies of leukemia.
1966 Bush is elected to U.S. House of Representatives.
1976 President Ford appoints Bush director of the Central Intelligence Agency (CIA).
1980 Bush is elected vice president and serves two terms with Ronald Reagan as president.
1988 Bush is elected president.
1989 Bush sends U.S. troops into Panama to oust its corrupt leader, General Manuel Noriega;

THE GULF WAR

In August, 1990, Iraq's leader, Saddam Hussein, ordered the invasion of his oil-rich neighbor Kuwait. When Saddam refused to withdraw his troops, George Bush coordinated a military coalition of U.S. and allied forces against him. In January, 1991, a sustained bombing campaign—Operation Desert Storm—was launched against Iraq from Saudi Arabia. Six weeks later, the Iraqis were driven out of Kuwait. Bush had shown himself as a dynamic world leader.

BARBARA BUSH

Barbara Bush devoted her White House years to the cause of literacy. She avoided the controversies that plagued many other first ladies by remaining silent about sensitive political issues that would interfere with her husband's policies. Mrs. Bush has written books to support reading programs nationwide as well as a best-selling autobiography. She is only the second woman in U.S. history to have both a husband and son, George W. Bush, serve as president. The first was Abigail Adams.

Barbara Bush with First Dog Millie

BIOGRAPHY

★ **YEARS AS FIRST LADY** 1989–1993
★ **BORN** Bronx, N.Y., June 8, 1925
★ **MARRIED** Rye, N.Y., Jan. 6, 1945
★ **CHILDREN** George Walker, Robin, John Ellis, Neil Mallon, Marvin Pierce, Dorothy

KEY EVENTS

the Berlin Wall, which separated East and West Berlin for 28 years, is torn down; Bush appoints Colin Powell chairman of the U.S. Joint Chiefs of Staff, the first African-American to hold this office.
1990 Iraq invades Kuwait; Germany is reunified; economic recession begins in the United States.
1991 United States and allies launch Operation Desert Storm and drive Iraq out of Kuwait; the Soviet Union breaks up; the Cold War ends.
1992 Bush signs the Earth Pledge, requiring limited emissions of greenhouse gases and eco-friendly development; Bush is defeated by Bill Clinton in the presidential election.

CLINTON

WILLIAM JEFFERSON CLINTON enjoyed a time of peace and prosperity as president. He signed debt reduction legislation and oversaw major reform of the nation's welfare system. In 1998, the Clinton administration passed the first balanced budget in almost 30 years. The economy prospered with high levels of home ownership and a low unemployment rate. Clinton's second term was marred by the Monica Lewinsky scandal, but this failed to diminish his high job-performance ratings.

FOREIGN AFFAIRS

Clinton negotiated the successful North American Free Trade Agreement with Canada and Mexico, and secured peace in Haiti by reinstating ousted president Jean-Bertrand Aristide. Clinton sent U.S. troops as part of NATO operation to war-torn Kosovo, a region in the former Yugoslavia. He also played a leading role in trying to bring peace in the Middle East between the Palestinians and Israelis, though a lasting peace has yet to be formed.

BIOGRAPHY

★ **42ND PRESIDENT**
1993–2001
★ **BORN** Hope, Ark.,
Aug. 19, 1946
★ **INAUGURATED AS PRESIDENT** First term:
Jan. 20, 1993
Second term:
Jan. 20, 1997
★ **PARTY** Democratic

KEY EVENTS

1973 William Jefferson Clinton and Hillary Rodham graduate from Yale Law School.
1975 Clinton and Rodham marry.
1976 Clinton becomes attorney general of Arkansas.

1978 Clinton is elected governor of Arkansas for one term and then defeated.
1982 Clinton is reelected governor of Arkansas and serves three terms.
1992 Clinton is elected president with Al Gore as

vice president.
1993 Clinton signs the North American Free Trade Agreement; Hillary Clinton heads task force on national healthcare reform; Israelis and Palestinians sign an agreement over disputed land.

CLINTON CONFESSES

In 1997, Clinton was faced with allegations concerning his relationship with 21-year-old White House intern Monica Lewinsky. Although Clinton initially denied the allegations, he was eventually forced to admit to a grand jury that he had indeed had an "inappropriate relationship" with Lewinsky. Impeachment proceedings on charges of perjury and obstruction of justice followed in January 1999. A month later, Clinton was acquitted.

HILLARY RODHAM CLINTON

No first lady has has such an active role in politics as Hillary Rodham Clinton. Educated in the 1960s, a time when women made great strides professionally and politically, Clinton was the first presidential spouse who continued her career after marriage. She was a well-respected lawyer in Arkansas with an interest in children's issues. With her election to the U.S. Senate in the year 2000, she also became the first one to hold a national office. Hillary had an ambitious view of her role as first lady, and her husband shared it, appointing her head of a task force to reform the U.S. health care system.

BIOGRAPHY

★ **YEARS AS FIRST LADY** 1993–2001
★ **BORN** Park Ridge, Ill., Oct. 26, 1947
★ **MARRIED** Fayetteville, Ark., Oct. 11, 1975
★ **CHILDREN** Chelsea

Senate campaign button

KEY EVENTS

1994 U.S. troops are withdrawn from Somalia; Nelson Mandela is elected president of South Africa; the Republicans win control of Congress.
1995 Bomb destroys federal building in Oklahoma City, killing hundreds.
1996 Clinton orders missile strikes on Iraq; Clinton is reelected.
1997 Monica Lewinsky scandal erupts.
1998 U.S. joins NATO operation to prevent ethnic cleansing in Kosovo; Clinton is impeached by Congress.
1999 Congress acquits Clinton; NATO bombs Serbia; Serbia withdraws from Kosovo.
2000 Hillary Rodham Clinton is elected U.S. senator from New York.

87

BUSH

GEORGE W. BUSH entered the White House after defeating Al Gore in a close and controversial presidential election. As president, Bush initiated a tax cut for all Americans. On September 11, 2001, terrorist attacks on New York City and Washington, D.C. prompted Bush to refocus his entire administration on investigating the crimes, bolstering national security, and planning a retaliatory course of action.

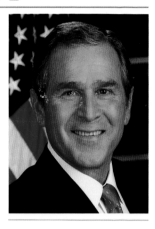

BIOGRAPHY

★ 43RD PRESIDENT 2001–
★ BORN New Haven, Ct., July 6, 1946
★ INAUGURATED AS PRESIDENT Jan. 20, 2001
★ PARTY Republican

LAURA BUSH
Before her marriage, Laura Welch taught school and earned a degree in library science. After her twin daughters were born, she devoted her time to their care. She worked on education and literacy projects as first lady of Texas. Now in the White House, she continues to focus on education and family issues.

BIOGRAPHY

★ YEARS AS FIRST LADY 2001–
★ BORN Midland, Tex., Nov. 4, 1946
★ MARRIED Midland, Tex., Nov. 5, 1977
★ CHILDREN Barbara, Jenna

KEY EVENTS

1973 Laura Welch receives a master's degree in library science from the University of Texas and works as a librarian.
1975 George W. Bush receives an M.B.A. from Harvard Business School.

1977 Bush and Welch marry.
1994 Bush is elected governor of Texas.
1998 Bush is reelected governor of Texas.
2000 Al Gore wins the popular vote but loses in the electoral college;

the Supreme Court halts a recount of votes in Florida; Gore concedes the election.
2001 Bush signs a tax cut; World Trade Center and Pentagon are attacked in the worst terrorist assault in U.S. history.

Presidents' Religious Affiliations

EPISCOPALIAN
George Washington
James Madison
James Monroe
William Henry
  Harrison
John Tyler
Zachary Taylor
Franklin Pierce
Chester A. Arthur
Franklin D. Roosevelt
Gerald R. Ford
George Bush

PRESBYTERIAN
Andrew Jackson
James Buchanan
Grover Cleveland
Benjamin Harrison
Woodrow Wilson
Dwight D. Eisenhower

METHODIST
James K. Polk
Ulysses S. Grant
Rutherford B. Hayes
William McKinley
George W. Bush

BAPTIST
Warren G. Harding
Harry S. Truman
Jimmy Carter
William Jefferson
  Clinton

UNITARIAN
John Adams
John Quincy Adams
Millard Fillmore
William H. Taft

DISCIPLES OF CHRIST
James A. Garfield
Lyndon B. Johnson
Ronald Reagan

NO FORMAL AFFILIATION
Thomas Jefferson
Abraham Lincoln
Andrew Johnson

DUTCH REFORMED
Martin Van Buren
Theodore Roosevelt

QUAKER
Herbert Hoover
Richard M. Nixon

CONGREGATIONALIST
Calvin Coolidge

ROMAN CATHOLIC
John F. Kennedy

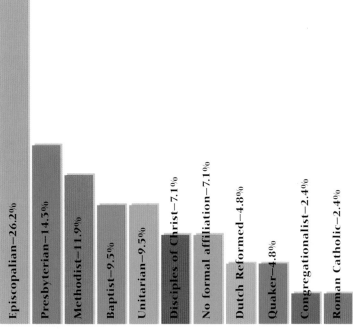

Episcopalian—26.2%
Presbyterian—14.5%
Methodist—11.9%
Baptist—9.5%
Unitarian—9.5%
Disciples of Christ—7.1%
No formal affiliation—7.1%
Dutch Reformed—4.8%
Quaker—4.8%
Congregationalist—2.4%
Roman Catholic—2.4%

PERCENT OF TOTAL NUMBER OF PRESIDENTS

IOWA
Mamie Eisenhower
Herbert Hoover
Lou Hoover

NEVADA
Pat Nixon

NEBRASKA
Gerald R. Ford

CALIFORNIA
Richard M. Nixon

TEXAS
Laura Bush
Dwight D. Eisenhow
Lady Bird Johnson
Lyndon B. Johnson

President and First Lady
Birthplaces by State

LONDON, ENGLAND
Louisa Adams

NEW YORK
Barbara Bush
Frances Cleveland
Abigail Fillmore
Millard Fillmore
Jacqueline Kennedy
Elizabeth Monroe
Nancy Reagan
Eleanor Roosevelt
Franklin D. Roosevelt
Theodore Roosevelt
Julia Tyler
Hannah Van Buren
Martin Van Buren

VERMONT
Chester A. Arthur
Calvin Coolidge
Grace Coolidge

NEW HAMPSHIRE
Franklin Pierce
Jane Pierce

MASSACHUSETTS
Abigail Adams
John Adams
John Quincy Adams
George Bush
John F. Kennedy

ILLINOIS
Hillary Rodham
   Clinton
Betty Ford
Ronald Reagan

CONNECTICUT
George W. Bush
Edith Roosevelt

NEW JERSEY
Grover Cleveland
Anna Harrison

MISSOURI
Julia Grant
Bess Truman
Harry S. Truman

TENNESSEE
Eliza Johnson
Sarah Polk

PENNSYLVANIA
James Buchanan
Harriet Lane

ARKANSAS
William Jefferson
   Clinton

NORTH CAROLINA
Andrew Johnson
Dolley Madison
James K. Polk

MARYLAND
Margaret Taylor

SOUTH CAROLINA
Andrew Jackson

VIRGINIA
Ellen Arthur
William Henry
   Harrison
Rachel Jackson
Martha Jefferson
Thomas Jefferson
James Madison
James Monroe
Zachary Taylor
John Tyler
Letitia Tyler
George Washington
Martha Washington
Edith Wilson
Woodrow Wilson

GEORGIA
Jimmy Carter
Rosalynn Carter
Ellen Wilson

KENTUCKY
Abraham Lincoln
Mary Lincoln

OHIO
James A. Garfield
Lucretia Garfield
Ulysses S. Grant
Florence Harding
Warren G. Harding
Benjamin Harrison
Caroline Harrison
Lucy Hayes
Rutherford B. Hayes
Ida McKinley
William McKinley
Helen Taft
William H. Taft

YEAR	CANDIDATES	POLITICAL PARTIES	POPULAR VOTE	ELECTORAL COLLEGE VOTE
1789	George Washington	Federalist	No record	69
	John Adams	Federalist		34
1792	George Washington	Federalist	No record	132
	John Adams	Federalist		77
1796	John Adams	Federalist	No record	71
	Thomas Jefferson	Democratic–Republican		68
1800*	Thomas Jefferson	Democratic–Republican	No record	73
	Aaron Burr	Democratic–Republican		73
	John Adams	Federalist		65
	Charles C. Pinckney	Federalist		64
1804	Thomas Jefferson	Democratic–Republican	No record	162
	Charles C. Pinckney	Federalist		14
1808	James Madison	Democratic–Republican	No record	122
	Charles C. Pinckney	Federalist		47
1812	James Madison	Democratic–Republican	No record	128
	DeWitt Clinton	Federalist		89
1816	James Monroe	Democratic–Republican	No record	183
	Rufus King	Federalist		34
1820	James Monroe	Democratic–Republican	No record	231
	John Quincy Adams	National–Republican		1
1824**	John Quincy Adams	National–Republican	108,740	84
	Andrew Jackson	Democratic–Republican	153,544	99
	Other candidates		93,754	78
1828	Andrew Jackson	Democratic	647,286	178
	John Quincy Adams	National-Republican	508,064	83
1832	Andrew Jackson	Democratic	688,242	219
	Henry Clay	National-Republican	473,462	49
1836	Martin Van Buren	Democratic	765,483	170
	William Henry Harrison	Whig	735,651	73
1840	William Henry Harrison	Whig	1,274,624	234
	Martin Van Buren	Democratic	1,127,781	60
1844	James K. Polk	Democratic	1,338,464	170
	Henry Clay	Whig	1,300,097	105
1848	Zachary Taylor	Whig	1,360,967	163
	Lewis Cass	Democratic	1,222,342	127
	Martin Van Buren	Free Soil	291,263	

YEAR	CANDIDATES	POLITICAL PARTIES	POPULAR VOTE	ELECTORAL COLLEGE VOTE
1852	Franklin Pierce	Democratic	1,601,117	254
	Winfield Scott	Whig	1,385,453	42
1856	James Buchanan	Democratic	1,832,955	174
	John C. Frémont	Republican	1,339,932	114
	Millard Fillmore	American	871,731	8
1860	Abraham Lincoln	Republican	1,865,593	180
	John C. Breckinridge	Democratic	848,356	72
	Stephen A. Douglas	Democratic	1,382,713	12
1864	Abraham Lincoln	Republican	2,206,938	212
	George B. McClellan	Democratic	1,803,787	21
1868	Ulysses S. Grant	Republican	3,013,421	214
	Horatio Seymour	Democratic	2,706,829	80
1872	Ulysses S. Grant	Republican	3,596,745	286
	Horace Greeley	Democratic	2,843,446	0
1876***	Rutherford B. Hayes	Republican	4,036,572	185
	Samuel J. Tilden	Democratic	4,284,020	184
1880	James A. Garfield	Republican	4,453,295	214
	Winfield S. Hancock	Democratic	4,414,082	155
1884	Grover Cleveland	Democratic	4,879,507	219
	James G. Blaine	Republican	4,850,293	182
1888	Benjamin Harrison	Republican	5,477,129	233
	Grover Cleveland	Democratic	5,537,857	168
1892	Grover Cleveland	Democratic	5,555,426	277
	Benjamin Harrison	Republican	5,182,690	145
1896	William McKinley	Republican	7,102,246	271
	William J. Bryan	Democratic	6,492,559	176
1900	William McKinley	Republican	7,218,491	292
	William J. Bryan	Democratic	6,356,734	155
1904	Theodore Roosevelt	Republican	7,628,461	336
	Alton B. Parker	Democratic	5,084,223	140
1908	William H. Taft	Republican	7,675,320	321
	William J. Bryan	Democratic	6,412,294	162
1912	Woodrow Wilson	Democratic	6,296,547	435
	Theodore Roosevelt	Progressive	4,118,571	88
	William H. Taft	Republican	3,486,720	8
1916	Woodrow Wilson	Democratic	9,127,695	277
	Charles E. Hughes	Republican	8,533,507	254
1920	Warren G. Harding	Republican	16,143,407	404
	James M. Cox	Democratic	9,130,328	127
1924	Calvin Coolidge	Republican	15,718,211	382
	John W. Davis	Democratic	8,385,283	136
1928	Herbert Hoover	Republican	21,391,993	444
	Alfred E. Smith	Democratic	15,016,169	87

YEAR	CANDIDATES	POLITICAL PARTIES	POPULAR VOTE	ELECTORAL COLLEGE VOTE
1932	Franklin D. Roosevelt	Democratic	22,809,638	472
	Herbert Hoover	Republican	15,758,901	59
1936	Franklin D. Roosevelt	Democratic	27,752,869	523
	Alfred M. Landon	Republican	16,674,665	8
1940	Franklin D. Roosevelt	Democratic	27,307,819	449
	Wendell L. Wilkie	Republican	22,321,018	82
1944	Franklin D. Roosevelt	Democratic	25,606,585	432
	Thomas E. Dewey	Republican	22,014,745	99
1948	Harry S. Truman	Democratic	24,179,345	303
	Thomas E. Dewey	Republican	21,991,291	189
1952	Dwight D. Eisenhower	Republican	33,936,234	442
	Adlai E. Stevenson	Democratic	27,314,992	89
1956	Dwight D. Eisenhower	Republican	35,590,472	457
	Adlai E. Stevenson	Democratic	26,022,752	73
1960	John F. Kennedy	Democratic	34,226,731	303
	Richard M. Nixon	Republican	34,108,157	219
1964	Lyndon B. Johnson	Democratic	43,129,566	486
	Barry M. Goldwater	Republican	27,178,188	52
1968	Richard M. Nixon	Republican	31,785,480	301
	Hubert H. Humphrey	Democratic	31,275,166	191
1972	Richard M. Nixon	Republican	47,169,911	520
	George S. McGovern	Democratic	29,170,383	17
1976	Jimmy Carter	Democratic	40,830,763	297
	Gerald R. Ford	Republican	39,147,793	240
1980	Ronald Reagan	Republican	43,899,248	489
	Jimmy Carter	Democratic	35,481,432	49
1984	Ronald Reagan	Republican	54,455,075	525
	Walter Mondale	Democratic	37,577,185	13
1988	George Bush	Republican	48,901,046	426
	Michael Dukakis	Democratic	41,809,030	111
1992	William Jefferson Clinton	Democratic	44,908,233	370
	George Bush	Republican	39,102,282	168
1996	William Jefferson Clinton	Democratic	47,402,357	379
	Bob Dole	Republican	39,198,755	159
2000****	George W. Bush	Republican	50,455,156	271
	Albert Gore, Jr.	Democratic	50,992,335	266

* Because Jefferson and Burr tied in the Electoral College, the House of Representatives voted to decide the winner, who was Jefferson.

** Jackson won the popular vote, but did not have a large enough majority in the Electoral College. The House of Representatives voted to decide the winner and chose Adams.

*** Though Tilden won the popular vote, Hayes won the Electoral College and the election by vote of a special Congressional commission.

**** Though Gore won the popular vote, the Supreme Court halted a recount of votes in Florida, prompting Gore to concede; Bush won the Electoral College and the election.

Index

95

ACKNOWLEDGMENTS

Media Projects, Inc. and DK Publishing, Inc. offer their grateful thanks to:
Ellen Nanney and Robyn Bissette at the Smithsonian Institution; James Barber and Beverly Cox of the National Portrait Gallery; William L. Bird, Lisa Kathleen Graddy, and Edith P. Mayo of the National Museum of American History; William F. Draper and his staff; the following curators, archivists, and photography professionals from both presidential libraries and private institutions: Athena Angelos, Hanna Edwards, Anthony Guzzi, Harmony Haskins, Kate Long, Peter Newark, George Ochoa, Thomas Price, David Smolen, and Jessica Tyree. Special thanks to Amy Pastan.

Photography and Art Credits
(t = top; b = bottom; l = left; r = right; c = center; a = above)

Ansel Adams: 80. Art Archive: 8b. Corbis: 9t, 73, 88c. George Bush Presidential Library: 85. The Hermitage: Home of President Andrew Jackson, Nashville, TN: 23c. Imageworks: 1. James K. Polk Memorial Association, Columbia, TN: 4tl, 29cl, 29br. Library of Congress: 8cr, 14tl, 16bl, 18cr, 24c, 24c, 27tl, 36lc, 37, 41, 45, 46c, 47c, 51c, 52t, 57, 59cl, 61tc, 64, 69, 71. LBJ Library Photo by Robert Knudsen: 75. Monticello/Thomas Jefferson Memorial Foundation, Inc.: 13b. New Hampshire Historical Society: 33lc. National Postal Museum: 65. National Museum of American Art, Smithsonian Institution: 21tr, 35cr. National Museum of American History: 4cr, 4bl, 4br, 6c, 10b, 26cr, 31cl, 31cr, 41tr, 48lc, 49rc, 52c, 54tl, 58rc, 68c, 74rc, 74cl, 77tc, 87c. National Portrait Gallery: 3, 4tr, 6tr, 7tl, 7b, 9br, 10tr, 12lc, 16tr, 17cl, 18cl, 20tr, 22tr, 22c, 24tl, 25tr, 26cl, 28tl, 30, 32tl, 33tr, 34, 35tl, 38, 40tr, 42tl, 42rc, 43, 44lc, 46tl, 47tr, 48tr, 50t, 51t, 53, 55tl, 55tr, 59tr, 60, 62tr, 68tl, 70l, 76, 81cr, 82tl, 84. Peter Newark's Pictures: 18cr, 56c. Ronald Reagan Library: 83. Smithsonian Institution: 4bc, 11bl, 12cr, 14lb, 15cl, 15cr, 19tl, 19b, 20bl, 27cr, 32cr, 36tr, 39tr, 40lc, 44rc, 46tl, 49tl, 50c, 54rc, 55c, 58tc, 61cl, 62c, 63, 66tl, 66rc, 67, 70cb, 72c, 78lc, 82c. The White House: 77rc, 79, 87lc, 88tr. The White House Collection, courtesy White House Historical Association: 86. William F. Draper: 72tr

Cover Credits
Corbis: Todd Gipstein back b. John F. Kennedy Library: back flap. Library of Congress: l. National Portrait Gallery: back la, back ra. Smithsonian Institution: r